THE
ROOTS OF
ENDURANCE

OTHER BOOKS BY THE AUTHOR

The Supremacy of God in Preaching

Recovering Biblical Manhood and Womanhood:
A Response to Evangelical Feminism
(edited with Wayne Grudem)

What's the Difference?
Manhood and Womanhood Defined According to the Bible

Let the Nations Be Glad: The Supremacy of God in Missions

The Justification of God:
An Exegetical and Theological Study of Romans 9:1–23

The Purifying Power of Living by Faith in Future Grace

Desiring God: Meditations of a Christian Hedonist

A Hunger for God: Desiring God Through Fasting and Prayer

A Godward Life, Book One:
Savoring the Supremacy of God in All of Life

God's Passion for His Glory: Living the Vision of Jonathan Edwards

The Innkeeper

A Godward Life, Book Two:
Savoring the Supremacy of God in All of Life

The Legacy of Sovereign Joy:
God's Triumphant Grace in the Lives of Augustine, Luther, and Calvin

The Pleasures of God: Meditations on God's Delight in Being God

The Hidden Smile of God:
The Fruit of Affliction in the Lives of John Bunyan,
William Cowper, and David Brainerd

Seeing and Savoring Jesus Christ

The Dangerous Duty of Delight:
The Glorified God and the Satisfied Soul

The Misery of Job and the Mercy of God

Brothers, We are Not Professionals:
A Plea to Pastors for Radical Ministry

Counted Righteous in Christ:
Should We Abandon the Imputation of Christ's Righteousness?

Beyond the Bounds:
Open Theism and the Undermining of Biblical Christianity
(edited with Justin Taylor and Paul Kjoss Helseth)

the swans are not silent

BOOK THREE

the ROOTS *of* Endurance

Invincible Perseverance
in the Lives of John Newton,
Charles Simeon, and William Wilberforce

JOHN PIPER

CROSSWAY BOOKS

A PUBLISHING MINISTRY OF
GOOD NEWS PUBLISHERS
WHEATON, ILLINOIS

First printing, 2002

First printing, trade paperback edition, 2006

Printed in the United States of America

ISBN 13: 978-1-58134-814-9
ISBN 10: 1-58134-814-2

Library of Congress Cataloging-in-Publication Data
Piper, John, 1946-
  The roots of endurance: invincible perseverance in the lives of
John Newton, Charles Simeon, and William Wilberforce / John Piper.
    p. cm. — (The swans are not silent ; bk. 3)
  Includes bibliographical references and indexes.
  ISBN 13: 978-1-58134-427-1
  ISBN 10: 1-58134-427-9 (alk. paper)
  1. Newton, John, 1725-1807. 2. Simeon, Charles, 1759-1836.
3. Church of England—Clergy—Biography. 4. Wilberforce, William,
1759-1833. 5. Abolitionists—Great Britain—Biography. 6. Legislators—
Great Britain—Biography. I. Title.
BX5197 .P57   2002
283'.092'242—dc21   2002005324

DP		16	15	14	13	12	11	10	09	08	07
15	14	13	12	11	10	9	8	7	6	5	4	3	2

To
my grandfather
Elmer Albert Piper

who said,
when he was almost dead
and Daddy prayed for faith,
one word:
"Amen"

CONTENTS

A book by Richard Sibbes, one of the choicest of the Puritan writers, was read by Richard Baxter, who was greatly blessed by it. Baxter then wrote his Call to the Unconverted *which deeply influenced Philip Doddridge, who in turn wrote* The Rise and Progress of Religion in the Soul. *This brought the young William Wilberforce, subsequent English statesman and foe of slavery, to serious thoughts of eternity. Wilberforce wrote his* Practical Book of Christianity *which fired the soul of Leigh Richmond. Richmond, in turn, wrote* The Dairyman's Daughter, *a book that brought thousands to the Lord, helping Thomas Chalmers the great preacher, among others.*

ERNEST REISINGER
"EVERY CHRISTIAN A PUBLISHER"
FREE GRACE BROADCASTER
ISSUE 51, WINTER 1995, P. 18

PREFACE

One reason "the swans are not silent" is that they all knew "the roots of endurance." Charles Simeon (1759-1836) endured as a faithful, evangelical, Anglican vicar for fifty-four years in one parish through opposition so severe that his "pewholding" parishioners boycotted his services during the first twelve years. William Wilberforce (1759-1833) endured as a faithful evangelical member of the British House of Commons, battling relentlessly for thirty years for the first triumph over the African slave trade in 1807, and another twenty-six years (three days before he died) to see slavery itself declared illegal. John Newton (1725-1807) was himself one of those African slave-trading captains, but was saved by "Amazing Grace"—to which he wrote the hymn—and became one of the roots of endurance that nourished both Simeon and Wilberforce in their trials.

Even if you have never heard of them, I urge you to get to know them. Together they are three of the healthiest, happiest, most influential[1] Christians of the latter eighteenth and early nineteenth centuries. My overwhelming impression, after seeing their

---

[1] The influence of Newton is symbolized by the almost universal use of the hymn "Amazing Grace," which he wrote. Wilberforce's influence is summed up in the glorious triumph over the African slave trade in England. Simeon is less known. But consider these two testimonies. Lord Macaulay, who had graduated from Cambridge in 1822 when Simeon was in his prime at Trinity Church in Cambridge, wrote in 1844, looking back on Simeon's entire influence, "As to Simeon, if you knew what his authority and influence were, and how they extended from Cambridge to the most remote corners of England, you would allow that his real sway over the Church was far greater than that of any Primate [bishop]" (Arthur J. Tait, *Charles Simeon and His Trust* [London: Society for Promoting Christian Knowledge, 1936], p. 58). And Charles Smyth wrote, "[Simeon,] more than any other, inspired and promoted the 'Evangelical Revival in the second and third generation of its course'" (quoted by Arthur Pollard, "The Influence and Significance of Simeon's Work," in *Charles Simeon (1759-1833): Essays Written in Commemoration of His Bi-Centenary by Members of the Evangelical Fellowship for Theological Literature*, eds. Arthur Pollard and Michael Hennell [London: SPCK, 1959], p. 181).

lives woven together in preparation for this book, is the remarkable mental health they shared. Not that they were perfect or without dark seasons. But on the whole, they are extraordinary examples of deep and joyful maturity. Their lives—as one person said of Wilberforce—were fatal not only to immorality but to dullness.[2] There was an invincible perseverance because there was invincible joy.

So the song of these three swans is worthy of the story that I tell here for the third time to explain the title of this series, *The Swans Are Not Silent*. St. Augustine, the Bishop of Hippo in North Africa, retired in A.D. 430. He handed over his duties to his humble successor, Eraclius. At the ceremony, Eraclius stood to preach as the aged Augustine sat on his bishop's throne behind him. Overwhelmed by a sense of inadequacy in Augustine's presence, Eraclius said, "The cricket chirps, the swan is silent."[3] The assumption of this series of books is that he was wrong.

You are now reading Book Three in the series. Book One is *The Legacy of Sovereign Joy: God's Triumphant Grace in the Lives of Augustine, Luther, and Calvin* (Crossway Books, 2000), and Book Two is *The Hidden Smile of God: The Fruit of Affliction in the Lives of John Bunyan, William Cowper, and David Brainerd* (Crossway Books, 2001).

As in the first two books, each chapter here is based on a message that I gave at the annual Bethlehem Conference for Pastors, which this year (2002) marked its fifteenth anniversary. I choose the word "message" intentionally—not "sermons," since they are not expositions of Scripture, and not "lectures," because

---

[2] See p. 149.
[3] Peter Brown, *Augustine of Hippo* (Berkeley, CA: University of California Press, 1969), p. 408.

they are passionately personal and, at times, will taste like preaching. There is no attempt here at dispassionate distance from my subject matter. I have a goal, and it is not hidden. I long to endure to the end for the glory of Christ, and I want to help others do the same. I believe God has ordained the history of sustaining grace in the lives of his living and long-dead people as a means to that end. God-centered, Christ-exalting, Bible-saturated saints who have endured to the end are one of the roots of our own endurance.[4]

As I write this Preface I have just preached to my people several messages in which I pleaded with them to be "coronary Christians," not "adrenal Christians." Not that adrenaline is bad, I said; it gets me through lots of Sundays. But it lets you down on Mondays. The heart is another kind of friend. It just keeps on serving—very quietly, through good days and bad days, happy and sad, high and low, appreciated and unappreciated. It never says, "I don't like your attitude, Piper, I'm taking a day off." It just keeps humbly lub-dubbing along. It endures the way adrenaline doesn't.

Coronary Christians are like the heart in the causes they serve. Adrenal Christians are like adrenaline—a spurt of energy and then fatigue. What we need in the cause of social justice (for example, against racism and abortion), and the cause of world mis-

---

[4] There are enough academic remnants left in me to include even more of a disclaimer, and enough of the pastor in me to restrict it to a footnote and be unashamed: My historical efforts in these biographies lay claim to no comprehensiveness or originality of research. I lean heavily, but not totally, on secondary sources that I cite generously as a tribute and for verification. In search of God's providence and grace, I ransack the sources for evidences of what makes a person tick spiritually. So there are huge Christian assumptions that I bring to the task: for instance, that God exists and is involved in the lives of these men, and that the Bible is true and gives valid interpretations of experience, and so on. I do not give deep and broad attention to the wider historical setting and culture in which they lived. And the list of limitations could go on. The point is: I am a pastor reading and writing between sermon preparation, staff leadership, prayer meetings, building programs, church-planting efforts, and so forth. If academic historians say, "Farewell," I don't blame them. I only hope that what I write is true and helps people endure to the end.

sions (to plant churches among the unreached peoples of the world), and the cause of personal holiness and evangelism (to lead people to Christ and love them no matter what) is not spurts of energy, but people who endure for the long haul. Marathoners, not sprinters.

I believe that reading about the lives of these three "coronary Christians" will help us endure to the end and finish well. Perhaps we will learn and experience what William Wilberforce discovered in his unwavering battle against the African slave trade: "I daily become more sensible that my work must be affected by constant and regular exertions rather than by sudden and violent ones."[5] May God be merciful in our day to multiply such coronary Christians for the cause of Christ and his kingdom.

---

[5] John Pollock, *Wilberforce* (London: Constable and Company, 1977), p. 116.

ACKNOWLEDGMENTS

For all the elders and ministers and support staff of Bethlehem Baptist Church I give public thanks. What a gift they are to me! Carried on the wings of prayer day by day I do my happy work. Yes, there are hard days and low seasons. But I say with Paul, "sorrowful, yet always rejoicing" (2 Corinthians 6:10). And largely because of these praying, hard-working, ever-encouraging friends. I could not be a pastor at Bethlehem *and* write if it were not for them.

At Desiring God Ministries, Justin Taylor is the kind of theological assistant who comes into a life like Halley's comet, once every seventy-six years or so. I thank God that Justin's orbit passed through my solar system at such a time as this. Vicki Anderson absorbs a hundred things that would land on me weekly and make my writing impossible. I thank God for her administrative excellence to be there for me in relation to so many good people. And special thanks to Carol Steinbach and Tamika Burns for the text and person indexes. I know, Carol, that preparing indexes is not *special* after doing so many, but it was, for you, a special year. Life is hard and God is good.

The backbone of this book was formed in preparation for the Bethlehem Conference for Pastors. The human key to that Conference is Jon Bloom. Without him, no conference. Without a conference, no book. So thanks again, Jon, for all the years of loving pastors with me.

Believing in this series and encouraging me along the way

has been Lane Dennis, President of Crossway Books. Your friendship, Lane, is a precious gift to Noël and me. And speaking of
Noël, she just read the whole manuscript in the last two days
and made dozens of wise suggestions. So I do not tire of singing
your praises, my good wife.

Finally, I thank God for my grandfather, Pastor Elmer Albert
Piper. I have dedicated the book to him. With no formal theological education, he could quote most of the New Testament by
heart. "One generation shall commend your works to another,
and shall declare your mighty acts" (Psalm 145:4). By grace,
utter grace, I have good roots.

For you have need of endurance,
so that when you have done the will of God
you may receive what is promised.
HEBREWS 10:36

Here is a call for the endurance of the saints,
those who keep the commandments of God
and their faith in Jesus.
THE APOSTLE JOHN
REVELATION 14:12

Have the full assurance of hope until the end,
so that you may not be sluggish, but imitators
of those who through faith and patience
inherit the promises.
HEBREWS 6:11-12

INTRODUCTION

The Biblical Roots of Endurance

Perhaps it's because I am in my mid-fifties as I write this, but whatever the reason, my mind defaults to thoughts about endurance these days. I want to finish well for the glory of Christ. I want to die well. But I have seen too much quitting and falling and failing to take anything for granted. "Let anyone who thinks that he stands take heed lest he fall" (1 Corinthians 10:12).

But I don't think that's the main reason endurance returns so often to my mind. I think it is a combination of global anxiety and biblical urgency. We are unsettled by the world. It does not feel safe. It seems fragile and insecure. The twentieth century was a sequence of bloody nightmares from which we could not wake up—because we were not asleep.[1] The twenty-first century has begun with the shattering realization that there is no safe place on earth. Slowly, perhaps, many are wakening to the biblical view that "here we have no lasting city, but we seek the city that is to come" (Hebrews 13:14); that this world does not offer a "kingdom that cannot be shaken" (Hebrews 12:28); that we are "sojourners and exiles" (1 Peter 2:11); that we should "not be surprised at the fiery trial . . . as though something strange were happening to" us (1 Peter 4:12); that "there will be great earthquakes, and in various places famines and pestilences . . . [and] ter-

---

[1] One way to sober yourself with the horrific reality of evil in the twentieth century is to consult a website like "Freedom, Democracy, Peace; Power, Democide, and War" at www.hawaii.edu/powerkills/welcome.html (accessed last on 2-22-02) where the evidence is given for about 170,000,000 people being murdered by their own governments in the twentieth century, not counting the world wars and other lesser conflicts.

rors" (Luke 21:11); that "there will come times of difficulty . . . people will be . . . abusive . . . heartless . . . brutal . . . treacherous, reckless" (2 Timothy 3:1-4).

The Unbiblical Absolutes of Self-Protection

There is a mind-set in the prosperous West that we deserve pain-free, trouble-free existence. When life deals us the opposite, we have a right not only to blame somebody or some system and to feel sorry for ourselves, but also to devote most of our time to coping, so that we have no time or energy left over for serving others.

This mind-set gives a trajectory to life that is almost universal—namely, away from stress and toward comfort and safety and relief. Then within that very natural trajectory some people begin to think of ministry and find ways of serving God inside the boundaries set by the aims of self-protection. Then churches grow up in this mind-set, and it never occurs to anyone in such a community of believers that choosing discomfort, stress, and danger might be the right thing—even the normal, biblical thing—to do.

I have found myself in conversation with Christians for whom it is simply a given that you do not put yourself or your family at risk. The commitment to safety and comfort is an unquestioned absolute. The demands of being a Christian in the twenty-first century will probably prove to be a rude awakening for such folks. Since we have not embraced the Calvary road voluntarily, God may simply catapult us onto it as he did the home-loving saints in Acts 11:19: "Those who were scattered *because of the persecution* that arose over Stephen traveled as far as Phoenicia and Cyprus and Antioch, speaking the word."

Stress and Danger Are Normal

One way or the other, Christ will bring his church to realize that "in the world you will have tribulation" (John 16:33); that "all who desire to live a godly life in Christ Jesus will be persecuted" (2 Timothy 3:12); that we are called to "share in suffering for the gospel by the power of God" (2 Timothy 1:8); that "we . . . groan inwardly as we wait eagerly for adoption as sons, the redemption of our bodies" (Romans 8:23); that "whoever would save his life will lose it, but whoever loses his life for [Christ's] sake and the gospel's will save it" (Mark 8:35); and that "through many tribulations we must enter the kingdom of God" (Acts 14:22).

If we will not freely take our cross and follow Jesus (Mark 8:34) on the Calvary road, it may be thrust on us. It would be better to hear the warnings now and wake up to biblical reality. Existence in this fallen world will not be pain-free and trouble-free. There will be groaning because of our finitude and fallenness, and many afflictions because of our calling (Romans 8:23; Psalm 34:19). Frustration is normal, disappointment is normal, sickness is normal. Conflict, persecution, danger, stress—they are all normal. The mind-set that moves away from these will move away from reality and away from Christ. Golgotha was not a suburb of Jerusalem.

Christians Move Toward Need, Not Comfort

For the apostle Paul, following Christ meant bearing the marks of his suffering. "We are treated as impostors, and yet are true; as unknown, and yet well known; as dying, and behold, we live; as punished, and yet not killed; as sorrowful, yet always rejoicing; as poor, yet making many rich; as having nothing, yet possessing everything" (2 Corinthians 6:8-10). Being a Christian should mean that our trajectory is toward need, regardless of danger and discomfort and stress. In other words, Christians characteristically will make life choices that involve putting themselves and their families at temporal risk while enjoying eternal security. "Sorrowful, yet always rejoicing . . . having nothing, yet possessing everything."

The Biblical Urgency of the Call for Endurance

All of this raises the question of endurance. How can we keep on loving and serving people when life has so much pain and disappointment? What are the roots of endurance? The magnitude of this question in the real world is one reason endurance has such a prominent place in the New Testament. One of the great themes of the Bible could be summed up in the words "You have need of endurance" (Hebrews 10:36).[2] Or the banner flying over the whole Book could be, "Here is a call for the endurance of the saints" (Revelation 14:12).

It is not a small consideration, since Jesus said, "The one who endures to the end will be *saved*" (Matthew 24:13). And Paul said, "If we endure, we will also *reign* with him" (2 Timothy 2:12). And the writer to the Hebrews said, "We *share in Christ*, if indeed we hold our original confidence firm to the end" (Hebrews 3:14).

---

[2] For an extended treatment of the doctrine of perseverance, see Thomas R. Schreiner and Ardel B. Caneday, *The Race Set Before Us: A Biblical Theology of Perseverance and Assurance* (Downers Grove, IL: InterVarsity Press, 2001). For an old and standard classic see John Owen, *The Doctrine of the Saint's Perseverance Explained and Confirmed*, in *The Works of John Owen*, Vol. 11 (Edinburgh: The Banner of Truth Trust, 1965, orig. 1654).

Repeatedly we are commanded to "stand" in the face of opposition that would knock us down or lure us to fall down or bow down. "Take up the whole armor of God, that you may be able to with*stand* in the evil day, and having done all, to *stand firm*" (Ephesians 6:13). "*Stand firm* thus in the Lord, my beloved" (Philippians 4:1). "Brothers, *stand firm* and hold to the traditions that you were taught by us" (2 Thessalonians 2:15).

We are admonished, "Do not grow weary in doing good" (2 Thessalonians 3:13). "Continue in what you have learned and have firmly believed" (2 Timothy 3:14). "Let us hold fast the confession of our hope without wavering" (Hebrews 10:23). "Hold fast what you have until I come" (Revelation 2:25). A blessing is pronounced on those who endure under trial. "Blessed is the man who remains steadfast under trial, for when he has stood the test he will receive the crown of life, which God has promised to those who love him" (James 1:12).

The assumption behind all these biblical texts is that the Christian life is hard. "The gate is narrow and the way is hard that leads to life" (Matthew 7:14); the Word of God can be "choked by the cares and riches and pleasures of life" (Luke 8:14); "your adversary the devil prowls around like a roaring lion, seeking someone to devour" (1 Peter 5:8); and "there are many adversaries" (1 Corinthians 16:9).

Therefore the danger is real that professing Christians will simply grow weary in well doing (Galatians 6:9); that we will fail to take heed to ourselves (1 Timothy 4:16) and each other (Hebrews 3:13; 10:24-25); and that we will just drift through life (Hebrews 2:1) and fail to see that there is a fight to be fought and a race to be won (1 Timothy 6:12; 2 Timothy 4:7).

How My Mind Has Changed

As I complete my fiftieth year as a professing Christian I feel the urgency of endurance more than ever. I used to think differently. I used to think, when I was in my twenties and thirties, that sanctification had a kind of cumulative effect and that at fifty the likelihood of apostasy would be far smaller than at thirty or forty. In one sense this is true. Surely growth in grace and knowledge and faith helps us "no longer be children, tossed to and fro by the waves and carried about by every wind of doctrine" (Ephesians 4:14). I see more clearly now that even after years of such growth and stability, shocking coldness and even apostasies are possible. And I have known moments of horrifying blankness that made me realize my utter dependence on the mercies of God being new every morning.

Perseverance is a gift. That I will wake up and be a believer tomorrow morning is not finally and decisively owing to my will, but to God. I have known too many mornings on the precipice to think otherwise. That I have been snatched back every time is sheer mercy. The human will cannot be depended on, because in the crisis of faith it is precisely the will that is weak and falling. The question is: Who will seize it and bring it back to God in faith? More and more I love the candor and truth of the old hymn by Robert Robinson:

> *O to grace how great a debtor*
> *Daily I'm constrained to be!*
> *Let thy goodness like a fetter*
> *Bind my wandering heart to thee:*
> *Prone to wander, Lord, I feel it,*
> *Prone to leave the God I love;*

> *Here's my heart, O, take and seal it;*
> *Seal it for thy courts above.*[3]

Desperate Praying for Endurance

That is my cry: "Let your goodness, O God, bind my heart with a chain to you! Seal my will to yours with an unbreakable application of your eternal covenant." Is this the way Christians should pray? "Keep me! Preserve me! Defeat every rising rebellion! Overcome every niggling doubt! Deliver from every destructive temptation! Nullify every fatal allurement! Expose every demonic deception! Tear down every arrogant argument! Shape me! Incline me! Hold me! Master me! Do whatever you must do to keep me trusting you and fearing you till Jesus comes or calls." Should we pray for endurance like this?

Yes. It is the way the Lord taught us to pray. It's the way the psalmist prayed, and the way the apostle Paul prayed. When we pray, "Hallowed be your name . . . your will be done, on earth as it is in heaven" (Matthew 6:9-10), we are asking that God would cause his name to be reverenced and his will to be done.[4] We are asking for divine influence to move our hearts and the hearts of others from irreverence to reverence and from rebellion to joyful submission. We are admitting that without divine help, our hearts do not endure in reverence and obedience.

---

[3] Robert Robinson, "Come, Thou Fount of Every Blessing," in *The Worshipping Church* (Carol Stream, IL: Hope Publishing Company, 1990), p. 45.

[4] I stress this because for years I prayed the Lord's Prayer as if the first three petitions were a kind of acclamation of praise, and not a desperate plea for God to act. The Greek verb form used for the three verbs—your name "hallowed," your kingdom "come," your will "be done"— is called a third person imperative. We don't have such a thing in English. But you can see the significance of it by comparing the use of this construction in other places, for example, in the form of the verb for "be baptized" in Acts 2:38, "Repent and be baptized every one of you." It is clearly an exhortation here: "be baptized." Similarly in the Lord's Prayer we are "exhorting" God urgently to be hallowed. We want him to cause this to come about in the world and, for starters, in our own hearts.

The psalmists prayed in the same way. They pleaded that God would overcome their failing wills: "*Incline* my heart to your testimonies, and not to selfish gain!" (Psalm 119:36). In other words, the psalmist saw that he was "prone to wander" away from endurance and faithfulness, and pleaded with God to intervene and change his will when he started to love money more than truth. Similarly he prayed that God would *open* his eyes to see the compelling beauty of what was there in the Word (Psalm 119:18), and that God would *unite* his heart from all its divided allegiances (Psalm 86:11), and that God would *satisfy*[5] him with divine love, and so wean him off the world (Psalm 90:14). Without this kind of divine help nobody will endure to the end in love to Christ. That is why the apostle Paul prays this way for his people: "May the Lord *direct your hearts* to the love of God and to the steadfastness of Christ" (2 Thessalonians 3:5). If we are going to endure in faith and obedience, God must "direct our hearts" to Christ.

The Foundation of Prayer in Promised Grace

That kind of praying is rooted in the New Covenant promise of sovereign, sustaining grace—the hope that God himself has promised to keep his people. In other words, the command that we endure to the end is not only a command, but a creation of God. God commands it, and God gives it. That is the foundation of our asking for it. One of the most magnificent expressions of God's promise to help us endure is in Jeremiah 32:38-41.

---

[5] Notice that the four italicized words ("incline," "open," "unite," "satisfy") from these four texts (Psalm 119:36; 119:18; 86:11; 90:14) form an acronym: "IOU'S." I use this regularly as a reminder of how to pray for my own soul and for others.

And they shall be my people, and I will be their God. I will give them one heart and one way, that they may fear me forever, for their own good and the good of their children after them. I will make with them an everlasting covenant, that I will not turn away from doing good to them. And I will put the fear of me in their hearts, that they may not turn from me. I will rejoice in doing them good, and I will plant them in this land in faithfulness, with all my heart and all my soul.

Here is one of the most stunning and precious promises of sustaining grace in the Bible. This is the New Covenant promise of God's initiative to do for us what under the Old Covenant the Jewish people, by and large, were not enabled to do.[6] Must we endure to the end to be saved? Yes. And in this New Covenant, God promises, "I will put the fear of me in their hearts, that they may not turn from me" (Jeremiah 32:40). He promises to do *for* us what he commands *from* us. This is what marks the Christian

---

[6] Here are some other places where promises of the New Covenant are found: Deuteronomy 30:6, "And the LORD your God will circumcise your heart and the heart of your offspring, so that you will love the LORD your God with all your heart and with all your soul, that you may live." Jeremiah 31:31-33, "Behold, the days are coming, declares the LORD, when I will make a new covenant with the house of Israel and the house of Judah, not like the covenant that I made with their fathers on the day when I took them by the hand to bring them out of the land of Egypt, my covenant that they broke, though I was their husband, declares the LORD. But this is the covenant that I will make with the house of Israel after those days, declares the LORD: I will put my law within them, and I will write it on their hearts. And I will be their God, and they shall be my people." Ezekiel 11:19-20, "And I will give them one heart, and a new spirit I will put within them. I will remove the heart of stone from their flesh and give them a heart of flesh, that they may walk in my statutes and keep my rules and obey them. And they shall be my people, and I will be their God." Ezekiel 36:26-27, "And I will give you a new heart, and a new spirit I will put within you. And I will remove the heart of stone from your flesh and give you a heart of flesh. And I will put my Spirit within you, and cause you to walk in my statutes and be careful to obey my rules." The fulfillment of the New Covenant is in the work of Jesus Christ in dying for our sins and purchasing the benefits of the promises of the New Covenant: "This cup that is poured out for you is the *new covenant* in my blood" (Luke 22:20; 1 Corinthians 11:26). Hebrews 9:15, "Therefore he is the mediator of a *new covenant*, so that those who are called may receive the promised eternal inheritance, since a death has occurred that redeems them from the transgressions committed under the first covenant." Along with this redemption comes the blessing promised in the New Covenant of divine enabling for the endurance in faith that God commands. Hebrews 13:20-21, "Now may the God of peace who brought again from the dead our Lord Jesus, the great shepherd of the sheep, *by the blood of the eternal covenant*, equip you with everything good that you may do his will, *working in us that which is pleasing in his sight*, through Jesus Christ, to whom be glory forever and ever. Amen."

pursuit of endurance from all others. It has been purchased by the blood of Jesus Christ and promised to those who are his.

A Peculiar Kind of Striving

So the form of our endurance has a peculiar energy: We put out great effort to endure to the end, but we do it in a peculiar way, namely, in the strength that God supplies. Paul said it like this in Philippians 2:12-13, "Work out your own salvation with fear and trembling, for it is God who works in you, both to will and to work for his good pleasure." We work and we tremble at the magnitude of what is at stake in our endurance and what great obstacles there are in ourselves and in the world and in the devil. But we do not tremble with the anxiety of the abandoned. We are not abandoned. In all our striving, there is a deep restfulness of confidence, for we are striving not in our strength but God's. "Finally, be strong in the Lord and in the strength of his might" (Ephesians 6:10). Not our might, *his* might.

Yes, there is a fight to be fought and a race to be run. Paul leaves us no question about that:

> Do you not know that in a race all the runners compete, but only one receives the prize? So run that you may obtain it. Every athlete exercises self-control in all things. They do it to receive a perishable wreath, but we an imperishable. So I do not run aimlessly; I do not box as one beating the air. But I discipline my body and keep it under control, lest after preaching to others I myself should be disqualified.
> —1 Corinthians 9:24-27

But be careful in reading such texts. Oh, how easy it would

be to simply turn them into moral self-improvement programs that have nothing to do with the blood-bought, Spirit-wrought New Covenant promises of divine enabling received by faith in Christ.

The crucial Christian difference for Paul was that he believed all his running and fighting and body disciplining was a gift of grace purchased by Jesus Christ and received by faith in him so that Jesus would get the glory and not Paul himself. For example, Paul said, "By the grace of God I am what I am, and his grace toward me was not in vain. On the contrary, I worked harder than any of them, though it was not I, but the grace of God that is with me" (1 Corinthians 15:10). Yes, he worked to endure, but no, it was not finally and decisively dependent on him, but on the grace of God. "It depends not [finally and decisively] on human will or exertion, but on God, who has mercy" (Romans 9:16).

Enduring by Grace Through Faith So God Gets the Glory

The biblical call to endure in faith and obedience is a call to trust the Christ-purchased, empowering grace of God.[7] God's grace is first the gift of pardon and imputed righteousness;[8] then it is the gift of power to fight the good fight and to overflow in good deeds. Christ died to purchase both redeeming pardon *and* transforming power: "[Christ] gave himself for us to *redeem* us from all law-

---

[7] I have tried to spell this kind of living out in great biblical and practical detail in the book, *The Purifying Power of Living by Faith in FUTURE GRACE* (Sisters, OR: Multnomah Press, 1995).

[8] This term will become clearer in what follows, but in advance, it refers to the divine righteousness that God credits to our account on the basis of Christ's life and death. It is not what we do, but what God is and did in Jesus Christ. It is the basis of our acceptance with God. It is the foundation, not the effect, of our moral transformation that necessarily follows. As our sins were imputed to Christ who knew no sin, so God's righteousness is imputed to us who had no righteousness. 2 Corinthians 5:21, "For our sake he made him to be sin who knew no sin, so that in him we might become the righteousness of God." I have recently written a book defending and explaining the doctrine of imputed righteousness: *Counted Righteous in Christ: Should We Abandon the Imputation of Christ's Righteousness?* (Wheaton, IL: Crossway Books, 2002).

lessness and to *purify* for himself a people for his own possession who are zealous for good works" (Titus 2:14). Therefore, all our ability to endure to the end in good works is a gift of grace. This is what Paul says in 2 Corinthians 9:8: "God is able to make all grace abound to you, so that having all sufficiency in all things at all times, you may abound in every good work." Grace abounds to us so that we may abound in good works. It is our work, yes, but enabled by his grace.

That is why he gets the glory for our good works. Jesus called us to a life of good works, but in a peculiar way: namely, so that our Father, not ourselves, would get the glory: "Let your light shine before others, so that they may see your good works and give glory to your Father who is in heaven" (Matthew 5:16). This is exactly the way the apostle Peter reasoned in 1 Peter 4:11, "[Serve] by the strength that God supplies—in order that in everything God may be glorified through Jesus Christ. To him belong glory and dominion forever and ever. Amen."

The aim of all our endurance is that Christ be seen and savored in the world as our glorious God. Paul makes this plain in 2 Thessalonians 1:11-12 where he prays for us "that our God may make you worthy of his calling and may fulfill every resolve for good and every work of faith by his power, *so that the name of our Lord Jesus may be glorified in you*, and you in him, *according to the grace of our God* and the Lord Jesus Christ." Paul asks that God would energize all our resolves so that we would endure by the grace of God and for the glory of Christ, the image of God. Similarly, in Philippians 1:11 he prays that we would be "filled with the fruit of righteousness that comes through Jesus Christ, to the glory and praise of God." He asks God to fill us with the fruit of righteousness because of the work of Jesus Christ, and that in this way God would see to it that he himself gets the glory.

This is what we pray for, and this is what we trust in as we take up the biblical command to endure to the end. We trust in the New Covenant promises of sustaining, enabling grace that were obtained for us infallibly and irrevocably by Jesus Christ in his death and resurrection. Therefore our fight and our race and endurance is a radically God-centered, Christ-exalting, Spirit-dependent, promise-supported life. It is not a "just do it" ethic. It is not a moral self-improvement program. It is not a "Judeo-Christian ethic" shared by a vaguely spiritual culture with a fading biblical memory. It is a deeply cross-embracing life that knows the Christ of the Bible as the Son of God who was crucified first as our substitute and then as our model of endurance.

Pardon Before Power

Nothing was more important for John Newton, Charles Simeon, and William Wilberforce than the centrality of the cross as the root of endurance. They did exactly what Hebrews 12:1-2 calls us to do: "Let us run with *endurance* the race that is set before us, *looking to Jesus*, the founder and perfecter of our faith, who for the joy that was set before him *endured the cross*." They endured . . . looking to Jesus . . . who endured the cross.

But oh how jealous they were—as I am jealous—that we embrace the cross of Christ first and decisively as the ground of our acceptance with God, through faith alone, *before* we experience the cross as the price and inspiration of our own labors to endure in the battle for justice in the world. That is, they were

careful to savor the cross first as the basis of justification before
they experienced its purchased power for sanctification. *Before* the
power of endurance came the pardon of guilt. *Before* the blood-
bought enabling of righteous living came the free gift of perfect
righteousness credited to our account because of Christ alone
through faith alone.

The Politician Who Cared Deeply about Doctrine

Astonishingly William Wilberforce, the politician who had no formal theological training at all, was more explicit and urgent about
this matter than either of the two pastors, Newton or Simeon. As
he endured decade after decade in the battle against the African
slave trade, he came to an amazing diagnosis of the problem. His
nominally Christian, British countrymen did not understand justification by faith in its proper, foundational relation to sanctification. They were confusing the two.

First, they considered doctrine as ethically unimportant. They
had what he called "the fatal habit"—and surely we in the prosperous, pragmatic West would have to admit that it is even more
habitual today—"of considering Christian morals as distinct from
Christian doctrines. . . . Thus the peculiar doctrines of Christianity
went more and more out of sight, and as might naturally have
been expected, the moral system itself also began to wither and
decay, being robbed of that which should have supplied it with life
and nutriment."[9] The central "peculiar doctrine" that went out
of sight with worst effect was a true understanding of justification by faith.

---

[9] William Wilberforce, *A Practical View of Christianity* (Peabody, MA: Hendrickson Publishing
Company, 1996), p. 198.

What was it particularly that was lost? Here is how he put it in 1797: The errors and moral failures of the mass of nominal Christians

> RESULT FROM THE MISTAKEN CONCEPTION ENTERTAINED OF THE FUNDAMENTAL PRINCIPLES OF CHRISTIANITY. They consider not that Christianity is a scheme "for justifying *the ungodly*" [Romans 4:5], by Christ's dying for them "*when yet sinners*" [Romans 5:6-8], a scheme "for reconciling us to God—*when enemies* [Romans 5:10]; and for making the fruits of holiness *the effects, not the cause*, of our being justified and reconciled.[10]

This is the root of endurance in true godliness that was lost. And the effect in the culture was devastating. Nominal Christians were confusing and reversing sanctification and justification. They were making the fruits of holiness the cause and not the effects of being justified.

In other words, they were cutting themselves off from the very power of justification by faith that was the deepest root of life and power that the Bible offers for defeating sin and freeing us for lifelong endurance in the cause of righteousness. Wilberforce returns again to this theme with these clear and powerful words: "The true Christian . . . knows therefore that this holiness is not to PRECEDE his reconciliation to God, and be its CAUSE; but to FOLLOW it, and be its EFFECT. That, in short, it is by FAITH IN CHRIST only that he is to be justified in the sight of God."[11] In this way alone does a person become "entitled to all the privileges which belong to this high relation," which include in this earthly life a

---

[10] Ibid., p. 64. The capitalization and italics are his emphasis.
[11] Ibid., p. 166. His capitalization.

"partial renewal after the image of his Creator," and in the life to come "the more perfect possession of the Divine likeness."[12]

The deepest root of endurance for Wilberforce—and Newton and Simeon shared this view entirely—was the precious and powerful experience of the justification of the *ungodly* by faith alone (Romans 4:5)—leading necessarily to a life of glorious freedom in the never-ending battle against sin and injustice. Any effort to short-circuit this process of faith in Christ for his imputed righteousness first, and transformed morality second, would in the end be the undoing of morality and of a nation.

The Surprising Place of Cross-Focused Doctrine

This discovery in William Wilberforce and Charles Simeon surprised me. I did not expect to find a politician decrying the decay of doctrinal knowledge as the root of failed endurance in righteous living. All I knew when I took up the study of Wilberforce was that he had an unparalleled reputation for Christian endurance in the cause of justice for African slaves. That is what I wanted to understand.[13] And all I knew of Charles Simeon when I began to study his life was that he had served in one university church for fifty-four years, and in the first twelve years there was such vigorous opposition to his ministry from his people that the "pewholders" (as they were called in those days) would not let anyone sit in the pews, so that he had to preach to an audience

---

[12] Ibid.

[13] The 2002 Bethlehem Conference for Pastors was built around this issue of racial justice and the foundation for it in God-centered thinking. Messages from that conference are available through Desiring God Ministries, www.desiringGOD.org or 1-888-346-4700.

standing in the space that was left. I wanted to understand how one endures so long under such relentless opposition.

I did not realize that both of these men would make the cross of Christ so vital to the root of their endurance, and that Wilberforce in particular would focus on the very nature of justification as the linchpin of endurance in righteous living. I knew Newton somewhat better before I began a more thorough study of his life. Everyone knows his tribute to "Amazing Grace" that saved a "wretch" like me. So I expected what I found in Newton—overflowing grace for the worst of sinners grounded in the finished and perfect work of Jesus Christ on the cross. So there is a continuity in these three men at the deepest level, not just at the experiential level of lifelong endurance against all obstacles. They are united in their delight in and devotion to the cross of Christ as the ground of God's righteousness freely imputed to them through faith alone as the root of all righteous endurance.

And the Surprising Place of Cross-Focused Delight

The word "delight" is chosen carefully. This was another surprise in studying the lives of these three men. I did not expect the aggressive way that they made joy essential to Christian living and long endurance through pain. It was not a general, vague joy, but a specific, focused joy in the cross and in the Christ who died for us there. For example, Simeon said, "By this then, my brethren, you may judge whether you are Christians in deed and in truth, or such in name only. For a nominal Christian is content with *proving* the way of salvation by a crucified Redeemer. But the true Christian loves it, *delights* in it, glories in it, and shudders at the very thought of glorying in anything else."[14] Delight in the Christ of the cross, not just dutiful endurance, was essential for all three of these men. It is—as we will see—one of the essential roots of endurance.

The Linking of Three Lives

There are several ways to think about the interrelatedness of Newton (1725-1807), Simeon (1759-1836), and Wilberforce (1759-1833). They were contemporaries who knew and respected each other. Their lives were interwoven in a common cause of evangelical reformation. The first two were local church pastors and the third a member of the House of Commons all his life. All had drunk deeply at the wells of George Whitefield and John Wesley. Simeon and Wilberforce were the same age and Newton their senior by thirty-four years. Therefore, the role of Newton in these relationships was of father and counselor and encourager—which was his well-known and cherished gift. In a sense, then, Newton *was* a root of their renowned endurance.

Newton's Wise Nurture of William Wilberforce

Already as a boy, Wilberforce knew John Newton. The aunt and uncle with whom he stayed for long periods after his father died when he was eight were friends of Newton and listened to him often. Therefore Newton watched Wilberforce's career from the time he was a boy and grieved over his worldly wanderings before his conversion at age twenty-six. But when Wilberforce was powerfully converted—a great story of God's surprising providence

---

[14] Charles Simeon, *Evangelical Preaching: An Anthology of Sermons by Charles Simeon* (Sisters, OR: Multnomah Press, 1986), p. 71. Italics added.

that we will see in Chapter 3—it was John Newton to whom he turned for counsel about whether he could remain in public political life as an evangelical. In the history of the world, more hung on that private meeting of December 7, 1785, than we know.

Wilberforce reported, "He told me he always had hopes and confidence that God would sometime bring me to Him. . . . When I came away I found my mind in a calm, tranquil state, more humbled, and looking more devoutly up to God."[15] But more important historically than the peace of Wilberforce's soul that day was the counsel he received about political life as an evangelical. Newton told him to stay in politics. "It is hoped and believed that the Lord has raised you up for the good of His church and for the good of the nation."[16]

And till the day Newton died in 1807, he was Wilberforce's cheerleader. Or, more biblically, he was like a Moses on the mountain to Joshua on the field doing battle with Amalek. Wilberforce wrote him in 1788:

> I believe I can truly declare, that not a single day has passed in which you have not been in my thoughts. . . . O my dear Sir, let not your hands cease to be lifted up, lest Amalek prevail—entreat for me that I may be enabled by divine grace to resist and subdue all the numerous enemies of my salvation. My path is peculiarly steep and difficult and dangerous, but the prize is a crown of glory and "celestial panoply" is offered me and the God of Hosts for my ally.[17]

---

[15] Robert Isaac Wilberforce and Samuel Wilberforce, *The Life of William Wilberforce*, abridged edition (London, 1843), p. 48.

[16] Ibid. This quote is from a letter Newton wrote two years later, but it sums up what Wilberforce said he received from Newton that day. Similarly Newton wrote to Wilberforce in 1799 concerning the entire "Clapham Sect"—the like-minded group of friends who lived near each other and fought the same battles, "But when I think of you, Mr. Thornton and a few of your friends, I am ready to address you in the words of Mordecai—who knoweth but God raised you up for such a time as this!" Richard Cecil, *The Life of John Newton*, ed. Marylynn Rouse (Fearn, Ross-shire, Great Britain: Christian Focus Publications, 2000), p. 177.

[17] Ibid., pp. 176-177.

The Blessing Returned on Newton's Head

Though Newton was older and more seasoned and the one
Wilberforce looked to for wise counsel,[18] Newton learned from
and honored his younger "Joshua." In 1797 when Wilberforce
published his one main, nation-shaping book—the one that diag-
nosed Britain's ills as rooted in the doctrinal failure to grasp justification by faith—Newton told him that he read it three times
in the first two months after it came out. "I have been nearly fifty
years in the Lord's school . . . but still I had something to learn
from your book."[19] He was not slack in honoring the accom-
plishments of Wilberforce far and near. He once said that he
believed Britain owed to Wilberforce the "pleasing prospect of
an opening for the gospel in the southern Hemisphere." In fact, six
years after Newton's death, because of Wilberforce's relentless
advocacy, liberty to preach the Gospel finally came to the British
colonies as far away as India.[20]

Another Young Beneficiary of Newton's Amazing Grace

The relation between Newton and Charles Simeon was not as
close, but they knew each other, and Newton admired the young

---

[18] Newton nurtured and sustained Wilberforce's endurance with regular letters (at least four a
year by his own telling). A taste of this nurture: "My heart is with you, my dear sir. I see,
though from a distance, the importance and difficulties of your situation. May the wisdom
that influenced Joseph and Moses and Daniel rest upon you. Not only to guide and animate
you in the line of Political Duty—but especially to keep you in the habit of dependence upon
God, and communion with him, in the midst of all the changes and bustle around you." Ibid.,
p. 176.

[19] Wilberforce, *A Practical View of Christianity*, p. 263.

[20] The British citizen and missionary William Carey, who went to India in 1793, had to live in
a Danish enclave in Serampore, India, until Wilberforce finally triumphed in 1813 (six years
after Newton died). The prohibition of evangelism in British areas of India was lifted by the East
India Company Charter, and liberty was granted to propagate the Christian Faith. "Parliament
had opened a fast-locked door and it was Wilberforce who had turned the key, in a speech which
Lord Erskine said 'deserves a place in the library of every man of letters, even if he were an
atheist.'" John Pollock, *Wilberforce* (London: Constable, 1977), p. 238.

vicar of Trinity Church, Cambridge. He knew of his long endurance and wrote of him, "There is good going on at Cambridge. Mr. Simeon is much beloved and very useful; his conduct has almost suppressed the spirit of opposition which was once very fierce against him."[21] The ordeal that Simeon had endured at Trinity Church was known far and wide. Even Wilberforce, years after the battles had been won in Cambridge, wrote to Simeon in 1829, "The degree in which, without any sacrifice of principle, you have been enabled to live down the prejudices of many of our high ecclesiastical authorities, is certainly a phenomenon I never expected to witness."[22]

Tribute to the Little-Known Emissaries of Sustaining Grace

Typical of the interweaving of these men's lives was one other brief but all-important link between Simeon and Wilberforce. Isaac Milner, the man who led Wilberforce to Christ during several months of travel together in France, was a close friend of Simeon in Cambridge. First as a tutor and then principal of Queens' College in the university, Milner became a strong supporter of Simeon in his trials. Thus a relatively unknown person in history may have played a role in the lives of Simeon and Wilberforce beyond anything we know. It is fitting that such a one be mentioned here as a kind of tribute to all the unknown emissaries of grace God sends to us in time of need.

---

[21] Richard Cecil, *The Life of John Newton*, p. 173.
[22] Handley C. G. Moule, *Charles Simeon* (London: InterVarsity Fellowship, 1948, orig. 1892), p. 152.

Gratitude That These Three Swans Are Still Not Silent

This book and this whole series of books, The *Swans Are Not Silent*, is a kind of debt I owe to people living and dead whom God mercifully sends my way to strengthen my hand in the fight of faith. I said at the start of this Introduction that I want to finish life well for the glory of Christ. One of the "roots of endurance" that I depend on is the life and ministry of men and women whose God-centered, Christ-exalting, cross-focused perseverance inspires me to press on through hardship. The Bible encourages me in this: "[Do] not be sluggish, but imitators of those who through faith and patience inherit the promises" (Hebrews 6:12). "As an example of suffering and patience . . . take the prophets. . . . You have heard of the steadfastness of Job, and you have seen the purpose of the Lord, how the Lord is compassionate and merciful" (James 5:10-11).

The twenty-first century will not be an easy time to be a Christian. It is not meant to be easy. But we are not left without help. The Bible centers on a crucified, risen, and reigning Christ and is full of promises for every crisis. And the history of God's church is full of empowering examples of those who proved that the grace of God is sufficient to enable us to endure to the end and be saved.

Amazing grace!—how sweet the sound
That saved a wretch like me,
I once was lost, but now am found,
Was blind, but now I see.

JOHN NEWTON

By faith he triumphs over . . . smiles and enticements:
he sees that all that is in the world,
suited to gratify the desires of the flesh or the eye,
is not only to be avoided as sinful,
but as incompatible with his best pleasures.

JOHN NEWTON

He believes and feels his own weakness and unworthiness,
and lives upon the grace and pardoning love of his Lord.
This gives him an habitual tenderness and gentleness of spirit.
Humble under a sense of much forgiveness to himself,
he finds it easy to forgive others.

JOHN NEWTON

1

JOHN NEWTON

The Tough Roots of His Habitual Tenderness

John Newton was born July 24, 1725, in London to a godly
mother and an irreligious, seafaring father. His mother died when
he was six. Left mainly to himself, Newton became a debauched
sailor—a miserable outcast on the coast of West Africa for two
years; a slave-trading sea-captain until an epileptic seizure ended
his career; a well-paid "surveyor of tides" in Liverpool; a loved
pastor of two congregations in Olney and London for forty-three
years; a devoted husband to Mary for forty years until she died
in 1790; a personal friend to William Wilberforce, Charles
Simeon, Henry Martyn, William Carey, John Wesley, and George
Whitefield; and, finally, the author of the most famous hymn in the
English language, "Amazing Grace."[1] He died on December 21,
1807, at the age of eighty-two.

---

[1] Besides appearing in almost all church hymnals, "'Amazing Grace' has been adapted by scores
of performers, from country music to gospel to folk singers. . . . Judy Collins sings in St. Paul's
Chapel at Columbia University, and talks about how this song carried her through the depths
of her alcoholism. Jessye Norman sends 'Amazing Grace' soaring across the footlights at
Manhattan Center stage. While in Nashville, Johnny Cash visits a prison and talks about the
hymn's impact on prisoners. The folk singer, Jean Ritchie, shares a reunion of her extended
family in Kentucky where everyone rejoices together. 'Amazing Grace' is also featured in the
repertory of the Boys Choir of Harlem, which performs the hymn in both New York and Japan"
(www.wlu.ca/mtr/MediaCollection/A/v1396.htm [accessed 1-26-2001]).

Durable as Redwoods, Tender as Clover

Why am I interested in this man? Because one of my great desires is to see Christians be as strong and durable as redwood trees, and as tender and fragrant as a field of clover—unshakably rugged in the "defense and confirmation" of the truth (Philippians 1:7) and relentlessly humble and patient and merciful in dealing with people. Ever since I came to Bethlehem Baptist Church as preaching pastor in 1980, this vision of ministry has beckoned me because, soon after I came, I read through Matthew and Mark and put in the margin of my Greek New Testament a "TO" (for tough) and a "TE" (for tender) beside Jesus' words and deeds that fit one category or the other. The impact on me was significant in shaping the course of my work. What a mixture he was! No one ever spoke like this man.

It seems to me that we are always falling off the horse on one side or the other in this matter of being tough and tender, durable and delightful, courageous and compassionate—wimping out on truth when we ought to be lionhearted, or wrangling when we ought to be weeping. I know it's a risk to take up this topic and John Newton in a cultural situation like ours where some readers need a good (tender!) kick in the pants to be more courageous and others confuse courage with what William Cowper called "a furious and abusive zeal."[2] Oh, how rare are the Christians who speak with a tender heart and have a theological backbone of steel.

I dream of being one someday, and I long to be used by God in the ministry to produce such fruit. Oh, for Christians and pas-

---

[2] Richard Cecil, *Memoirs of the Rev. John Newton*, in *The Works of the Rev. John Newton*, Vol. 1 (Edinburgh: The Banner of Truth Trust, 1985), p. 123.

tors whose might in the truth is matched by their meekness. Whose theological acumen is matched by their manifest contrition. Whose heights of intellect are matched by their depths of humility. Yes, and the other way around!—whose relational warmth is matched by their rigor of study, whose bent toward mercy is matched by the vigilance of their biblical discernment, and whose sense of humor is exceeded by the seriousness of their calling.

I dream of durable, never-say-die defenders of true doctrine who are mainly known for the delight they have in God and the joy in God that they bring to the people of God—who enter controversy when necessary, not because they love ideas and arguments, but because they love Christ and the church.

Lovers of Doctrine Who Spread Joy

There's a picture of this in Acts 15. Have you ever noticed the amazing unity of things here that we tend to tear apart? A false doctrine arises in Antioch; some begin to teach, "Unless you are circumcised . . . you cannot be saved" (verse 1). Paul and Barnabas weigh in with what Luke calls "no small dissension and debate" (verse 2). So the church decides to send them off to Jerusalem to get the matter settled. And amazingly, verse 3 says that on their way to the great debate they were "describing in detail the conversion of the Gentiles, and brought *great joy* to all the brothers" (verse 3, italics added).

This is my vision: The great debaters on their way to a life-and-death showdown of doctrinal controversy, so thrilled by the mercy and power of God in the Gospel that they are spreading joy everywhere they go. Oh, how many there are today who tell us that controversy only kills joy and ruins the church; and how many others there are who, on their way to the controversy, feel no joy and spread no joy in the preciousness of Christ and his salvation. One of the aims of my life and this book is to declare that it is possible and necessary to be as strong and rugged for truth as a redwood and as tender and fragrant for Christ as a field of clover.

No Perfect Pastors

So now, with the help of the life of John Newton, I want to say it again. And make no mistake—our heroes have feet of clay. There are no perfect Christians—laypeople or pastors. Newton himself warns us:

> In my imagination, I sometimes fancy I could [create] a perfect minister. I take the eloquence of _____, the knowledge of _____, the zeal of _____, and the pastoral meekness, tenderness, and piety of _____. Then, putting them all together into one man, I say to myself, "This would be a perfect minister." Now there is One, who, if he chose to, could actually do this; but he never did it. He has seen fit to do otherwise, and to divide these gifts to every man severally as he will.[3]

So neither Newton nor we will ever be all that we should be in this life. But oh, how much more like the Great Shepherd we should long to be. Newton had his strengths, and I want us to learn from them. At times his strengths were his weakness, but that too will be instructive. The theme of this chapter is "the tough

---

[3] Ibid., p. 107.

roots of John Newton's habitual tenderness." His great strength was "speaking the truth in love" (Ephesians 4:15). As you read, read for what *you* need, not for what so-and-so across town needs. On which side of the horse are *you* falling off?

I begin with a brief telling of his life, because for Newton, his life was the clearest testimony to the heart-breaking mercy of God he ever saw. Even at the end of his life he was still marveling that he was saved and called to preach the Gospel of grace. From his last will and testament we read:

> I commit my soul to my gracious God and Savior, who mercifully spared and preserved me, when I was an apostate, a blasphemer, and an infidel, and delivered me from the state of misery on the coast of Africa into which my obstinate wickedness had plunged me; and who has been pleased to admit me (though most unworthy) to preach his glorious gospel.[4]

This was one of the deepest roots of his habitual tenderness. He could not get over the wonder of his own rescue by sheer, triumphant grace.

His Childhood and Youth

Newton's mother was a devout Congregationalist and taught her only child, John, the Westminster Catechism and the hymns of Isaac Watts. But she died in 1732 when John was six, and his father's second wife had no spiritual interest. Newton wrote in his *Narrative* that he was in school only two of all his growing-

---

[4] Ibid., p. 90.

up years, from ages eight to ten, at a boarding school in Stratford. So he was mainly self-taught, and that remained true all his life. He never had any formal theological education.[5]

At the age of eleven he began to sail the high seas with his father. He made five voyages to the Mediterranean before he was eighteen. He wrote about his relationship to his father: "I am persuaded he loved me, but he seemed not willing that I should know it. I was with him in a state of fear and bondage. His sternness . . . broke and overawed my spirit."[6]

A Durable Romance

When he was seventeen he met Mary Catlett and fell in love with her. She was thirteen. For the next seven years of traveling and wretchedness he dreamed about her. "None of the scenes of misery and wickedness I afterwards experienced ever banished her a single hour together from my waking thoughts for the seven following years."[7] They did eventually marry when he was twenty-four, and were married for forty years until she died in 1790. His love for her was extraordinary before and after the marriage. Three years after she died, he published a collection of letters he had written to her on three voyages to Africa after they were married.

---

[5] In view of the fact that two of the three "Swans" in this book (Newton and Wilberforce) had no formal theological education, this might be a good place to encourage readers who, like these two great saints, have not been trained formally but who have drunk deeply at the wells of God's Word. Don't feel paralyzed in ministry and evangelism and eldership if you have not gone to seminary. Give yourself to reading and thinking and praying. There are many such lovers of God's truth who understand things and speak things as well as many seminary-trained pastors and teachers. I don't say this with any desire to diminish the value of formal training. I only want to say it is not essential for fruitful ministry if other ways of study and experience are seriously pursued.

[6] Ibid., p. 2.

[7] Ibid., p. 6.

Moral Ruin and Misery

He was pressed into naval service against his will when he was eighteen and sailed away bitterly on the *Harwich* as a midshipman. His friend and biographer Richard Cecil says, "The companions he met with here completed the ruin of his principles."[8] Of himself he wrote, "I was capable of anything; I had not the least fear of God before my eyes, nor (so far as I remember) the least sensibility of conscience. . . . My love to [Mary] was now the only restraint I had left."[9] On one of his visits home he deserted the ship and was caught, "confined two days in the guard-house . . . kept a while in irons . . . publicly stripped and whipt, degraded from his office."[10]

When he was twenty years old he was put off his ship on some small islands just southeast of Sierra Leone, West Africa, and for about a year and a half he lived as a virtual slave in almost destitute circumstances. The wife of his master despised him and treated him cruelly. He wrote that even the African slaves would try to smuggle him food from their own slim rations.[11] Later in life he marveled at the seemingly accidental way a ship put anchor on his island after seeing some smoke, and just happened to be a ship with a captain who knew Newton's father and managed to free him from his bondage.[12] That was February 1747. He was not quite twenty-one, and God was about to close in.

---

[8] Ibid., p. 9.
[9] Ibid., p. 12.
[10] Ibid., p. 10.
[11] Ibid., p. 16.
[12] Ibid., p. 78.

The Precious Storm at Sea

The ship had business on the seas for over a year. Then on March 21, 1748, on his way home to England in the North Atlantic, God acted to rescue the "African blasphemer."[13] On this day fifty-seven years later, in 1805, when Newton was eighty years old, he wrote in his diary, "March 21, 1805. Not well able to write. But I endeavor to observe the return of this day with Humiliation, Prayer and Praise."[14] He had marked the day as sacred and precious for over half a century.

He awoke that night to a violent storm as his room began to fill with water. As he ran for the deck, the captain stopped him and had him fetch a knife. The man who went up in his place was immediately washed overboard.[15] He was assigned to the pumps and heard himself say, "If this will not do, the Lord have mercy upon us."[16] It was the first time he had expressed the need for mercy in many years.

He worked the pumps from 3 in the morning until noon, slept for an hour, and then took the helm and steered the ship till midnight. At the wheel he had time to think back over his life and his spiritual condition. At about six o'clock the next evening it seemed as though there might be hope. "I thought I saw the hand of God displayed in our favor. I began to pray: I could not utter the prayer of faith; I could not draw near to a reconciled God, and call him *Father* . . . the comfortless principles of infidelity were deeply riveted. . . . The great question now was, how to obtain *faith*."[17]

---

[13] Ibid., p. 88.

[14] D. Bruce Hindmarsh, *John Newton and the English Evangelical Tradition* (Grand Rapids, MI: Eerdmans, 2001), p. 13.

[15] Cecil, *Memoirs of the Rev. John Newton*, p. 25.

[16] Ibid., p. 26.

[17] Ibid., p. 28.

He found a Bible and got help from Luke 11:13, which promises the Holy Spirit to those who ask. He reasoned, "If this book be true, the promise in this passage must be true likewise. I have need of that very Spirit, by which the whole was written, in order to understand it aright. He has engaged here to give that Spirit to those who ask: I must therefore pray for it; and, if it be of God, he will make good on his own word."[18]

He spent all the rest of the voyage in deep seriousness as he read and prayed over the Scriptures. On April 8 they anchored off Ireland, and the next day the storm was so violent they would have surely been sunk, had they still been at sea. Newton described what God had done in those two weeks:

> Thus far I was answered, that before we arrived in Ireland, I had a satisfactory evidence in my own mind of the truth of the Gospel, as considered in itself, and of its exact suitableness to answer all my needs. . . . I stood in need of an Almighty Savior; and such a one I found described in the New Testament. Thus far the Lord had wrought a marvelous thing: I was no longer an infidel: I heartily renounced my former profaneness, and had taken up some right notions; was seriously disposed, and sincerely touched with a sense of the undeserved mercy I had received, in being brought safe through so many dangers. I was sorry for my past misspent life, and purposed an immediate reformation. I was quite freed from the habit of swearing, which seemed to have been as deeply rooted in me as a second nature. Thus, to all appearance, I was a new man.[19]

---

[18] Ibid.
[19] Ibid., p. 32.

It was a remarkable change, but from his later mature stand-point, Newton did not view it as full conversion.

> I was greatly deficient in many respects. I was in some degree affected with a sense of my enormous sins, but I was little aware of the innate evils of my heart. I had no appre-hension of . . . the hidden life of a Christian, as it consists in communion with God by Jesus Christ: a continual dependence on him. . . . I acknowledged the Lord's mercy in pardoning what was past, but depended chiefly upon my own resolution to do better for the time to come. . . . I cannot consider myself to have been a believer (in the full sense of the word) till a considerable time afterwards.[20]

Captain, Epileptic, and Surveyor

For six years after this time he said he had no "Christian friend or faithful minister to advise me."[21] He became the captain of a slave-trading ship and went to sea again until December 1749. In his mature years he came to feel intense remorse for his partic-ipation in the slave trade and joined William Wilberforce in opposing it. Thirty years after leaving the sea he wrote an essay, *Thoughts upon the African Slave Trade*, which closed with a ref-erence to "a commerce so iniquitous, so cruel, so oppressive, so destructive, as the African Slave Trade!"[22]

On February 1, 1750, he married Mary. That June his father drowned while swimming in the Hudson Bay. John went on three long voyages after the marriage and left Mary alone for ten to thir-

---

[20] Ibid., pp. 32-33.
[21] Ibid., p. 33.
[22] John Newton, "Thoughts upon the African Slave Trade," in *The Works of the Rev. John Newton*, Vol. 6 (Edinburgh: The Banner of Truth Trust, 1985), p. 123.

teen months each time. Then in November 1754 he had an epileptic seizure and never sailed again.

Self-Taught

In the years between his seafaring and his pastorate at Olney he was a Surveyor of Tides in Liverpool and a very active ministerial layperson. He interacted with evangelicals from both the Anglican and Independent wings of the Awakening. He was especially taken by George Whitefield and "was even tagged with the epithet 'Little Whitefield' for his constant attendance upon the evangelist."[23] He devoted himself to a rigorous program of self-study and applied himself to Greek and Hebrew and Syriac. He said, "I was in some hopes that perhaps, sooner or later, [Christ] might call me into his service. I believe it was a distant hope of this that determined me to study the original Scriptures."[24]

Along with these he was reading "the best writers in divinity" in Latin and English and French (which he taught himself while at sea), but gave himself mainly to the Scriptures.[25] The upshot theologically of this study, together with his personal experience of grace, is summed up by Bruce Hindmarsh: "By the early 1760's Newton's theological formation was complete, and there

---

[23] D. Bruce Hindmarsh, "'I Am a Sort of Middle-Man': The Politically Correct Evangelicalism of John Newton," in *Amazing Grace: Evangelicalism in Australia, Britain, Canada, and the United States*, eds. George Rawlyk and Mark Noll (Grand Rapids, MI: Baker Book House, 1993), p. 32.

[24] Cecil, *Memoirs of the Rev. John Newton*, p. 50. Later in his ministry, Newton counseled a younger minister, "The original Scriptures well deserve your pains, and will richly repay them" (*The Works of the Rev. John Newton*, Vol. 1, p. 143). Concerning the early years of studying the languages he says, "You must not think that I have attained, or ever aimed at, a critical skill in any of these. . . . In the Hebrew, I can read the Historical Books and Psalms with tolerable ease; but, in the Prophetical and difficult parts, I am frequently obliged to have recourse to lexicons, etc. However, I know so much as to be able, with such helps as are at hand, to judge for myself the meaning of any passage I have occasion to consult" (Cecil, *Memoirs of the Rev. John Newton*, pp. 49-50).

[25] Ibid., p. 50.

would be few significant realignments of his essential beliefs. He was a five-point Calvinist."[26] But the spirit of his Calvinism was sweet and tender—as it should be!

Two Pastorates, No Children, and Heaven

In 1764 he accepted the call to the pastorate of the Church of England parish in Olney and served there for almost sixteen years. Then he accepted the call at age fifty-four to St. Mary's Woolnoth in London where he began his twenty-seven-year ministry on December 8, 1779. His eyes and ears were failing, and his good friend Richard Cecil suggested he cease preaching when he turned eighty, to which Newton responded, "What! Shall the old African blasphemer stop while he can speak?"[27] The last time he was in the pulpit of St. Mary's was in October 1806, when he was eighty-one years old.

John and Mary had no children of their own, but adopted two nieces. When Mary died seventeen years before John, he lived with the family of one of these nieces and was cared for by her as if he were her own father. He died on December 21, 1807, at the age of eighty-two. A month before he died he expressed his settled faith:

> It is a great thing to die; and, when flesh and heart fail, to have God for the strength of our heart, and our portion for-ever. I know whom I have believed, and he is able to keep that which I have committed against that great day. Henceforth there is laid up for me a crown of righteousness, which the Lord, the righteous Judge, shall give me that day.[28]

---

[26] Hindmarsh, "'I Am a Sort of Middle-Man,'" p. 42.
[27] Cecil, *Memoirs of the Rev. John Newton*, p. 88.
[28] Ibid., p. 89.

Newton's Habitual Tenderness

We turn now to the theme of this chapter, namely, "the tough roots of John Newton's habitual tenderness." This tenderness and these roots are seen in his remarkable pastoral ministry for over forty years.

The phrase "habitual tenderness" is Newton's own phrase to describe the way a believer should live. In writing to a friend he describes the believer's life: "He believes and feels his own weakness and unworthiness, and lives upon the grace and pardoning love of his Lord. This gives him an habitual tenderness and gentleness of spirit."[29] In that sentence, it is plain already what some of the roots of tenderness are, but before we look at them more closely let's get some snapshots of this man's "habitual tenderness."

It will be helpful to speak of persons and patterns. That is, to whom was he tender, and what form did his tenderness take?

Loving People at First Sight

Richard Cecil said, "Mr. Newton could live no longer than he could *love*."[30] His love to people was the signature of his life. This was true of groups of people and individual people. He loved perishing people, and he loved his own flock of redeemed people.

> Whoever . . . has tasted of the love of Christ, and has known, by his own experience, the need and the worth of redemption, is enabled, Yea, he is constrained, to love his fellow creatures. *He loves them at first sight*; and, if the

---

[29] *The Works of the Rev. John Newton*, Vol. 1, p. 170.
[30] Cecil, *Memoirs of the Rev. John Newton*, p. 95.

providence of God commits a dispensation of the gospel, and care of souls to him, he will feel the warmest emotions of friendship and tenderness, while he beseeches them by the tender mercies of God, and even while he warns them by his terrors.[31]

It's the phrase "at first sight" that stands out in this quote. Newton's first reflex was to love lost people. When he spoke to unbelievers, he spoke like this:

A well-wisher to your soul assures you, that whether you know these things or not, they are important realities. . . . Oh hear the warning voice! *Flee from the wrath to come.* Pray thee that the eyes of your mind may be opened, then you will see your danger, and gladly follow the shining light of the Word.[32]

Suffer the Little Children to Come

One clear mark of Christlike tenderness is love for children. "Let the little children come to me; do not hinder them" (Mark 10:14) is the badge of tenderness that Jesus wore. When Newton came to Olney, one of the first things he did was begin a meeting for children on Thursday afternoons. He met with them himself, gave them assignments, and spoke to them from the Bible. At one point he said, "I suppose I have 200 that will constantly attend."[33] And what made it more remarkable to his parish-

---

[31] *The Works of the Rev. John Newton,* Vol. 5, p. 132, emphasis added.

[32] Richard Cecil, *The Life of John Newton,* ed. Marylynn Rouse (Fearn, Ross-shire, Great Britain: Christian Focus Publications, 2000), p. 351, emphasis added. He had a special concern for sailors and lamented their neglect in evangelism and Christian publishing. He eventually wrote a preface for a devotional book designed especially for sailors. See Cecil, *The Life of John Newton,* pp. 76-77, 347-348. Note: Marylynn Rouse's name is misspelled on the cover of this book as Rousse, but is correct on the inside title page.

[33] Ibid., p. 143.

ioners was that the meetings were open to all the children, not just the members of his church.

Josiah Bull said, "The *young* especially had a warm place in his affectionate heart. . . . Mr. Jay . . . relates that once a little sailor-boy with his father called on Mr. Newton. He took the boy between his knees, told him that he had been much at sea himself, and then sang him part of a naval song."[34]

The Flocks

For forty-three years his two flocks had an especially tender place in his heart. Richard Cecil said that Newton's preaching was often not well prepared, nor careful or "graceful" in delivery. But, he said, "He possessed . . . so much affection for his people, and so much zeal for their best interests, that the defect of his manner was little consideration with his constant hearers."[35] Once Newton complained in a letter of his busyness: "I have seldom one-hour free from interruption. Letters that must be answered, visitants that must be received, business that must be attended to. I have a good many sheep and lambs to look after, sick and afflicted souls dear to the Lord; and *therefore, whatever stands still, these must not be neglected.*"[36]

Minister to the Depressed

Newton's tenderness touched individuals as well as groups. The most remarkable instance of this was, of course, William Cowper,

---

[34] Josiah Bull, *"But Now I See": The Life of John Newton* (Edinburgh: The Banner of Truth Trust, 1998, orig. 1868), pp. 336-367.

[35] Cecil, *Memoirs of the Rev. John Newton*, p. 92.

[36] Cecil, *The Life of John Newton*, p. 139, emphasis added.

the mentally-ill poet and hymn-writer who came to live in Olney during twelve of Newton's sixteen years there. Newton took Cowper into his home for five months during one season and fourteen months during another when he was so depressed it was hard for him to function alone. In fact, Richard Cecil said that over Newton's whole lifetime, "His house was an asylum for the perplexed or afflicted."[37] Newton says of Cowper's stay: "For nearly 12 years we were seldom separated for seven hours at a time when we were awake and at home: the first six I passed daily admiring and aiming to imitate him: during the second six, I walked pensively with him in the valley of the shadow of death."[38]

When Cowper's brother died in 1770, Newton resolved to help Cowper by collaborating with him in writing hymns for the church. These came to be known as "The Olney Hymns." But soon Cowper was emotionally unable to carry through his part of the plan. Newton pressed on, writing one hymn a week without Cowper until there were well over three hundred. Sixty-seven are attributed to William Cowper.[39] The last hymn that Cowper composed for *The Olney Hymns* was "God Moves in a Mysterious Way," which he entitled "Light Shining out of Darkness." The next day, in January 1773, he sank into the blackest depression and never went to hear Newton preach again. Newton preached his funeral sermon seven years later and explained what happened and how he responded.

> He drank tea with me in the afternoon. The next morning a violent storm overtook him. . . . I used to visit him

---

[37] Cecil, *Memoirs of the Rev. John Newton*, p. 95.
[38] Cecil, *The Life of John Newton*, p. 125.
[39] Ibid.

often but no argument could prevail with him to come and see me. He used to point with his finger to the church and say: "You know the comfort I have had there and how I have seen the glory of the Lord in His house, and until I go there I'll not go anywhere else." He was one of those who came out of great tribulations. He suffered much here for twenty-seven years, but eternity is long enough to make amends for all. For what is all he endured in this life, when compared with the rest which remaineth for the children of God.[40]

What would most of us have done with a depressed person who could scarcely move out of his house? William Jay summed up Newton's response: "He had the tenderest disposition; and always judiciously regarded his friend's depression and despondency as a physical effect, for the removal of which he prayed, but never reasoned or argued with him concerning it."[41]

Satan Will Not Love You for This

Another example of his tenderness toward an individual is the case of the missionary, Henry Martyn. The young Martyn was very discouraged from some criticism he had received of his "insipid and inanimate manner in the pulpit." He came to Newton, who blocked every one of Martyn's discouragements with hope. Martyn wrote in his journal (April 25, 1805) that when Newton heard of the criticism he had received,

He said he had heard of a clever gardener, who would sow seeds when the meat was put down to roast, and

---

[40] Ibid., pp. 129-130.
[41] Ibid., p. 282.

engage to produce a salad by the time it was ready, but
the Lord did not sow oaks in this way. On my saying that
perhaps I should never live to see much fruit; he answered
I should have the bird's-eye view of it, which would be
much better. When I spoke of the opposition that I should
be likely to meet with, he said, he supposed Satan would
not love me for what I was about to do. The old man
prayed afterwards with sweet simplicity.[42]

From Liberal to Lover of the Truth

Another instance of remarkable patience and tenderness was
toward Thomas Scott, who was a liberal, "nearly . . . Socinian"
clergyman in Ravenstone, a neighboring parish. Scott made jest of
Newton's evangelical convictions. He looked upon Newton's
religious sentiments as "rank fanaticism" and found his theology
unintelligible. "Once I had the curiosity to hear [Newton] preach;
and, not understanding his sermon, I made a very great jest of it,
where I could do it without giving offense. I had also read one of
his publications; but, for the same reason, I thought the greater
part of it whimsical, paradoxical, and unintelligible."[43]

But things were soon to change. Gospel-driven love triumphed
over liberalism and turned Scott into a strong evangelical preacher.
The turning point came when Scott was shamed by Newton's pastoral care for two of his own parishioners whom he had neglected.

In January, 1774 two of my parishioners, a man and his
wife, lay at the point of death. I had heard of the circum-
stance; but, according to my general custom, not being sent

---

[42] Ibid., p. 184.
[43] Ibid., p. 65.

for, I took no notice of it: till, one evening, the woman being now dead, and the man dying, I heard that my neighbor Mr. Newton had been several times to visit them. Immediately my conscience reproached me with being shamefully negligent, in sitting at home within a few doors of dying persons, my general hearers, and never going to visit them. Directly it occurred to me, that, whatever contempt I might have for Mr. Newton's doctrines, I must acknowledge his practice to be more consistent with the ministerial character than my own.[44]

Scott and Newton exchanged about ten letters between May and December 1775. Scott was impressed with how friendly Newton was, even when Scott was very provocative. Newton "shunned everything controversial as much as possible, and filled his letters with the most useful and least offensive instructions."[45] After a lull in their correspondence from December 1775 to April 1777, Scott came into "discouraging circumstances" and chose to call on the tenderhearted evangelical. "His discourse so comforted and edified me, that my heart, being by this means relieved from its burden, became susceptible of affection for him."[46] This affectionate relationship led Scott into the full experience of saving grace and evangelical truth. He became the pastor at Olney when Newton was called to London and wrote a distinctly evangelical book, *The Force of Truth*[47] and was among William Wilberforce's favorite preachers. Such were the persons and fruit of Newton's habitual tenderness.

Consider now the patterns of Newton's tenderness.

---

[44] Ibid., p. 64.
[45] Ibid., p. 66.
[46] Ibid., p. 67.
[47] Thomas Scott, *The Force of Truth* (Edinburgh: The Banner of Truth Trust, 1979, orig. 1779).

Not Driven Away or Carried Away

One way to describe the pattern of Newton's tenderness is to say that it was patient and perceptive. He captures this balance when he says, "Apollos met with two candid people in the church: they neither ran away because he was *legal*, nor were carried away because he was *eloquent*."[48] In other words, Newton was not driven away by people's imperfections, and he was not overly impressed by their gifts. He was patient and perceptive. He saw beneath the surface that repelled and the surface that attracted. He once wrote to a friend, "Beware, my friend, of mistaking the ready exercise of gifts for the exercise of grace."[49] Being gracious to people did not mean being gullible.

Defeating Heresy by Establishing Truth

The most illuminating way I know to illustrate Newton's deeply rooted habitual tenderness is in the way he handled doctrinal and moral truth that he cherished deeply. Here we see the very *roots* of the tenderness (truth) at work in the *fruit* of tenderness (love). Patience and perception guided him between doctrinaire intellectualism on the one side and doctrinal indifference and carelessness on the other side.

With respect to patience Newton said:

> I have been thirty years forming my own views; and, in the course of this time, some of my hills have sunk, and some of my valleys have risen: but, how unreasonable

---

[48] Cecil, *Memoirs of the Rev. John Newton*, p. 101.
[49] *The Works of the Rev. John Newton*, Vol. 1, p. 164.

within me to expect all this should take place in another person; and that, in the course of a year or two.[50]

He had a passion for propagating the truth, even the whole Reformed vision of God as he saw it. But he did not believe controversy served the purpose. "I see the unprofitableness of controversy in the case of Job and his friends: for, if God had not interposed, had they lived to this day they would have continued the dispute."[51] So he labored to avoid controversy and to replace it with positive demonstrations of biblical truth. "My principal method of defeating heresy is by establishing truth. One proposes to fill a bushel with *tares*: now, if I can fill it first with *wheat*, I shall defy his attempts."[52] He knew that receiving the greatest truths required supernatural illumination. From this he inferred that his approach should be patient and unobtrusive:

> I am a friend of peace; and being deeply convinced that no one can profitably understand the great truths and doctrines of the gospel any farther than he is taught of God, I have not a wish to obtrude my own tenets upon others, in a way of controversy; yet I do not think myself bound to conceal them.[53]

---

[50] Cecil, *Memoirs of the Rev. John Newton*, p. 101.

[51] Ibid., p. 106. In a letter to a friend he warned that if we do not look continually to the Lord, controversy will obstruct communion with God. "Though you set out in defense of the cause of God, if you are not continually looking to the Lord to keep you, it may become your own cause and awaken in you those tempers which are inconsistent with true peace of mind and will surely obstruct communion with God" (*The Works of the Rev. John Newton*, Vol. 1, pp. 273-274).

[52] Cecil, *Memoirs of the Rev. John Newton*, p. 100.

[53] *The Works of the Rev. John Newton*, Vol. 3, p. 303.

The Temper of Tenderness in Telling Truth

Newton had a strong, clear, Calvinistic theology. He loved the
vision of God in true biblical Calvinism. In the preface to *The
Olney Hymns*, he wrote, "The views I have received of the doctrines of grace are essential to my peace; I could not live com-
fortably a day, or an hour, without them. I likewise believe . . .
them to be friendly to holiness, and to have a direct influence
in producing and maintaining a gospel conversation; and therefore I must not be ashamed of them."[54] But he believed "that
the cause of truth itself may be discredited by an improper management." Therefore, he says, "The Scripture, which . . . teaches
us *what* we are to say, is equally explicit as to the *temper* and
Spirit in which we are to speak. Though I had knowledge of all
mysteries, and the tongue of an angel to declare them, I could
hope for little acceptance or usefulness, unless I was to speak
'in love.'"[55]

> Of all people who engage in controversy, we, who are
> called Calvinists, are most expressly bound by our own
> principles to the exercise of gentleness and moderation. . . .
> The Scriptural maximum, that "The wrath of man work-
> eth not the righteousness of God," is verified by daily
> observation. If our zeal is embittered by expressions of
> anger, invective, or scorn, we may think we are doing ser-

---

[54] Ibid.

[55] *The Works of the Rev. John Newton*, Vol. 5, p. 131. Newton took Ephesians 4:15 ("speaking the truth in love") as his inaugural text when he came to St. Mary's (*The Works of the
Rev. John Newton*, Vol. 5, pp. 126-136). Richard Cecil describes how this text was fleshed
out in Newton's ministry. "His zeal in propagating the truth . . . was not more conspicuous
than the tenderness of the spirit as to the manner of his maintaining and delivering it. He was
found *constantly speaking the truth in love; and in meekness instructing those that oppose
themselves, if God peradventure would give them repentance to the acknowledging of the
truth.* There was a gentleness, a candour, and a forbearance in him, that I do not recollect to
have seen in an equal degree among his brethren . . ." (Cecil, *Memoirs of the Rev. John Newton*,
p. 122).

vice to the cause of truth, when in re
bring it into discredit.[56]

He had noticed that one of the most "C
the New Testament called for tenderness and pa
nents, because the decisive work is God's:

> *And the Lord's servant must not be quarrelsome but kind*
> *to everyone, able to teach, patiently enduring evil, cor-*
> *recting his opponents with gentleness. God may perhaps*
> *grant them repentance leading to a knowledge of the truth,*
> *and they may escape from the snare of the devil, after being*
> *captured by him to do his will.*
>
> —2 Timothy 2:24-26

So, for the sake of repentance and knowledge of truth,
Newton's pattern of tenderness in doctrinal matters was to shun
controversy.

Commending Opponents to God in Prayer

The sovereignty of God in freeing people from error or from unbelief also made prayer central to Newton's pattern of tenderness. In
a letter about controversy, he wrote a friend:

> As to your opponent, I wish, that, before you set pen to paper
> against him, and during the whole time you are preparing
> your answer, you may commend him by earnest prayer to the
> Lord's teaching and blessing. This practice will have a direct
> tendency to conciliate your heart to love and pity him; and
> such a disposition will have a good influence upon every page

---

[56] *The Works of the Rev. John Newton*, Vol. 1, p. 271.

you write. . . . [If he is a believer,] in a little while you will meet in heaven; he will then be dearer to you than the nearest friend you have upon earth is to you now. Anticipate that period in your thoughts. . . . [If he is an unconverted person,] he is a more proper object of your compassion than your anger. Alas! "He knows not what he does." But you know who has made you to differ [1 Corinthians 4:7].[57]

His Calvinism Is Like Sugar in His Tea

Newton cared more about influencing people with truth for their good than winning debates. William Jay recounts how Newton described the place of his Calvinism. He was having tea one day with Newton. Newton said, "'I am more of a Calvinist than anything else; but I use my Calvinism in my writings and my preaching as I use this sugar'—taking a lump, and putting it into his tea-cup, and stirring it, adding, 'I do not give it alone, and whole; but mixed and diluted.'"[58] In other words, his Calvinism permeated all that he wrote and taught and served to sweeten everything. Few people like to eat sugar cubes, but they like the effect of sugar when it permeates in right proportion.

So Newton did not serve up the "five points" by themselves but blended them in with everything he taught. This way of flavoring life was essential to his pattern of tenderness that developed in dealing with people's doctrinal differences. Bruce Hindmarsh remarks, "It is not surprising, therefore, that he wrote principally biographies, sermons, letters, and hymnody—not treatises or polemical tracts, much less a 'body of divinity.'"[59]

---

[57] Ibid., p. 269.
[58] Hindmarsh, "'I Am a Sort of Middle-Man,'" p. 52.
[59] Ibid.

Misgivings about Newton's Approach

Did Newton strike the right balance of a patient, tenderhearted, noncontroversial pattern of ministry and a serious vigilance against harmful error? Perhaps rather than indict Newton in particular, we should speak generally about the possible weakness in his approach. For example, William Plummer has misgivings:

> The pious and amiable John Newton made it a rule never to attack error, nor warn his people against it. He said: "The best method of defeating heresy is by establishing the truth. One proposes to fill a bushel with tares; now if I can fill it first with wheat, I shall defeat his attempts." Surely the truth ought to be abundantly set forth. But this is not sufficient. The human mind is not like a bushel. It may learn much truth and yet go after folly. The effect of Mr. Newton's practice was unhappy. He was hardly dead till many of his people went far astray. Paul says: "Preach the word; be instant in season, out of season; reprove, rebuke, exhort with all long-suffering and doctrine" (2 Timothy 4:2). The more subtle, bitter, and numerous the foes of the truth are the more fearless and decided should its friends be. The life of truth is more important than the life of any man or any theories.[60]

Bruce Hindmarsh has misgivings at another level. "While it is no disgrace that Newton was more a pastor than a theologian, it is one of the most serious indictments of the English Evangelical Revival that it produced so few theologians of stature."[61] In other words, if our zeal for peace and conciliation and heartfelt affec-

---

[60] William S. Plummer, *THE CHRISTIAN, to which is added, FALSE DOCTRINES AND FALSE TEACHERS: How to Know Them and How to Treat Them* (Harrisonburg, VA: Sprinkle Publications, 1997), p. 22.

[61] Hindmarsh, "'I Am a Sort of Middle-Man,'" p. 53.

tion for God and for people creates a milieu in which rigorous, critical thinking and theology will not flourish, we may hurt the cause of Christ in generations to come while seeming to make the cause more pleasing now.

He Could Draw a Line

I am not sure that Newton is to be faulted on these counts, even if the general concern is legitimate. It is true that John Wesley wrote to him, "You appear to be designed by divine providence for an healer of breaches, a reconciler of honest but prejudiced men, and an uniter (happy work!) of the children of God."[62] But it is also true that the relationship with Wesley was broken off in 1762 because of the controversy, not over election or perseverance, but over perfectionism.[63]

It is true that Richard Cecil criticized his hero, saying "that he did not always administer consolation . . . with sufficient discrimination. His talent," he said, "did not lie in *discerning of spirits.*"[64] But it is also true that Newton was unwavering in his

---

[62] Ibid., p. 31.

[63] Ibid., p. 43. In Liverpool, fifty-one Methodists claimed instantaneous and entire sanctification. "While Newton had been able to suppress his differences with Wesley over predestination, the extent of the atonement, and final perseverance, he was not able to accept the behavior of Wesley's followers in the wake of the perfectionism revival. The claim to perfection, however hedged about by talk of grace, seemed in many cases no more than an enthusiastic self-righteousness that belied trusting wholly in the merits of Christ for redemption. Newton had earlier worked out a formula that would maintain evangelical solidarity with Arminians by saying, 'Though a man does not accord with my view of election, yet if he gives me good evidence, that *he* is *effectually called of God*, he is my brother' [*The Works of the Rev. John Newton*, Vol. 6, p. 199]. He could not, however, make any rapprochement with Wesley's growing stress upon perfectionism. The behavior of his followers raised the specter of a Pelagianism that lay outside his understanding of evangelical theology, unduly stressing human agency in salvation."

[64] Cecil writes, "I never saw him so much moved, as when any friend endeavored to correct his errors in this respect. His credulity seemed to arise from the consciousness he had of his own integrity; and from the sort of parental fondness which he bore to all his friends, real or pretended. I knew one, since dead, whom he thus described, while living: 'He is certainly an odd man, and has his failings; but he has great integrity, and I hope is going to heaven:' whereas, almost all who knew him thought the man should go first into the pillory!" (Cecil, *Memoirs of the Rev. John Newton*, pp. 94-95).

commitment to holiness and doctrinal fidelity and was used by God to bring Thomas Scott from the brink of Socinianism to solid Reformed Christianity.

Most pastors and laypeople cannot devote much of their time to blowing the trumpet for rigorous intellectual theology. They should see its usefulness and necessity and encourage its proper place. But they cannot be faulted that they mainly have flocks to love and hearts to change. Defending the truth is a crucial part of that, but it is not the main part. *Holding* the truth and *permeating* all our ministry with the greatness and sweetness of truth for the transformation of our people's lives is the main part of our ministry.

The Eye and Tongue of a Poet

One other aspect of the pattern of Newton's tenderness calls for attention. It is the language he used in making the truth winsome and healing. Newton had the eye and heart and tongue of a spiritual poet, and this gave his speech a penetrating power that many Reformed preachers desperately need. He wrote hymns and poems for his people and for special occasions. Instead of excessive abstraction in his preaching, there was the concrete word and illustration. Instead of generalizing, there was the specific bird or flower or apple or shabby old man.

He had an eye that saw everything as full of divine light for ministry to people. For example, in his diary for July 30, 1776, Newton describes his reactions while watching an eclipse of the moon.

> Tonight I attended an eclipse of the moon. How great, O Lord, are thy works! With what punctuality do the heav-

enly bodies fulfill their courses. . . . I thought, my Lord, of Thine eclipse. The horrible darkness which overwhelmed Thy mind when Thou saidst, "Why hast thou forsaken me?" Ah, sin was the cause—my sins—yet I do not hate sin or loathe myself as I ought.[65]

Oh, how we need Christians—especially preachers—with eyes like this. Seeing God and his ways everywhere in nature and life, then making our communications full of concreteness from daily life.

Newton's language was permeated by this concreteness. Most of us tend to gravitate to abstractions. We say, "Men tend to choose lesser pleasures and reject greater ones." But Newton says, "The men of this world are children. Offer a child an apple and bank note, he will doubtless choose the apple."[66] We say, "Men are foolish to fret so much over material things when they will inherit eternal riches." But Newton says:

> Suppose a man was going to New York to take possession of a large estate, and his [carriage] should break down a mile before he got to the city, which obliged him to *walk* the rest of the way; what a fool we should think him, if we saw him wringing his hands, and blubbering out all the remaining mile, "My [carriage] is broken! My [carriage] is broken!"[67]

This is not merely a matter of style. It is a matter of life and vitality. It is a sign to people that your mind is healthy, and it may be a means to their health. Unhealthy minds can only deal

---

[65] Cecil, *The Life of John Newton*, p. 134.
[66] Cecil, *Memoirs of the Rev. John Newton*, p. 107.
[67] Ibid., p. 108.

in abstractions and cannot get outside themselves to be moved by concrete, external wonders. We will never be tender toward our people if we merely communicate the heaviness of general concepts and theories rather than the specific stuff of the world in which they live. This kind of communication was part and parcel of his winsome, humble, compelling tenderness.

The Health of Natural Humor

And yes, there is a crucial place for humor in this pattern of tenderness—not the contrived levity of a "communicator" who knows how to work an audience—but the balanced, earthy experience of the way the world really is in its horror and humor. There would be more real laughter if there were more real tears.

"One day by a strong sneeze he shook off a fly which had perched upon his gnomon, and immediately said: 'Now if this fly keeps a diary, he'll write Today a terrible earthquake.'" At another time, when asked how he slept, he instantly replied, "I'm like a beef-steak—once turned, and I am done."[68] What these quips indicate is a healthy mind awake to the world and free from bondage to morose speculations or introspection. This kind of mental health is essential for a Christian to be a tender and winsome minister to the whole range of human experience.

I turn now to the roots of John Newton's habitual tenderness.

---

[68] Bull, "*But Now I See,*" p. 370. The meaning of "gnomon" in 1803, according to the *Shorter Oxford Dictionary*, included "nose." That is probably Newton's reference. "Striking illustrations, happy turns of thought, racy and telling expressions, often enriched Mr. Newton's extempore discourses" (Bull, p. 369). Another instance of Newton's humor is seen in a letter to Thomas Scott who became the Vicar in Olney when Newton left. Newton wrote to him, "Methinks I see you sitting in my old corner in the study. I will warn you of one thing. That room—(do not start)—used to be haunted. I cannot say I ever saw or heard anything with my bodily organs, but I have been sure there were evil spirits in it and very near me—a spirit of folly, a spirit of indolence, a spirit of unbelief, and many others—indeed their name is legion. But why should I say they are in your study when they followed me to London, and still pester me here?" (Cecil, *The Life of John Newton*, ed. Marylynn Rouse, p. 145).

Realism About the Limits of This Life

Few things will tend to make you more tender than to be much in the presence of suffering and death. "My course of study," Newton said, "like that of a surgeon, has principally consisted in walking the hospital."[69] His biblical assessment of the misery that he saw was that some, but not much, of it can be removed in this life. He would give his life to bring as much relief and peace for time and eternity as he could. But he would not be made hard and cynical by irremediable miseries like Cowper's mental illness.[70] "I endeavor to walk through the world as a physician goes through Bedlam [the famous insane asylum]: the patients make a noise, pester him with impertinence, and hinder him in his business; but he does the best he can, and so gets through."[71] In other words, his tender patience and persistence in caring for difficult people came, in part, from a very sober and realistic view of what to expect from this world. Life is hard, and God is good.

Just as we saw at the beginning, there are no perfect pastors or laypeople. This must not discourage us but only make us patient as we wait for the day when all things will be new. Newton gives beautiful, concrete expression to this conviction as he watches the dawn outside his window.

---

[69] Cecil, *Memoirs of the Rev. John Newton*, p. 100.

[70] See pp. 56-57. Another case of constitutional depression (as he judged it) besides Cowper's was that of Hannah Wilberforce. Newton wrote to her in a letter dated July 1764, "Things which abate the comfort and alacrity of our Christian profession are rather impediments than properly sinful, and will not be imputed to us by him who knows our frame, and remembers that we are but dust. Thus, to have an infirm memory, to be subject to disordered, irregular, or low spirits, are faults of the constitution, in which the will has no share, though they are all burdensome and oppressive, and sometimes needlessly so by our charging ourselves with guilt on their account. The same may be observed of the unspeakable and fierce suggestions of Satan, with which some people are pestered, but which shall be laid to him from whom they proceed, and not to them who are troubled and terrified, because they are forced to feel them" (Cecil, *The Life of John Newton*, p. 126).

[71] Ibid., p. 103.

The day is now breaking: how beautiful its appearance! how welcome the expectation of the approaching sun! It is this thought makes the dawn agreeable, that it is the presage of a brighter light; otherwise, if we expect no more day than it is this minute, we should rather complain of darkness, than rejoice in the early beauties of the morning. Thus the Life of grace is the dawn of immortality: beautiful beyond expression, if compared with the night and thick darkness which formerly covered us; yet faint, indistinct, and unsatisfying, in comparison of the glory which shall be revealed.[72]

This sober realism about what we can expect from this fallen world is a crucial root of habitual tenderness in the life of John Newton.

All-Pervasive Humility and Gratitude at Having Been Saved

This he comes back to more than anything as the source of tenderness. Till the day he died, he never ceased to be amazed that, as he said at age seventy-two, "such a wretch should not only be spared and pardoned, but reserved to the honor of preaching thy Gospel, which he had blasphemed and renounced . . . this is won-

---

[72] *The Works of the Rev. John Newton*, Vol. 1, p. 319. Another example of the limits of this age that make us patient with people's failings is the God-ordained necessity of temptations. He asks "why the Lord permits some of his people to suffer such violent assaults from the powers of darkness" (ibid., p. 226). "Though the Lord sets such bounds to [Satan's] rage as he cannot pass, and limits him both as to manner and time, he is often pleased to suffer him to discover his malice to a considerable degree; not to gratify Satan, but to humble and prove them; to show them what is in their hearts, to make them truly sensible of their immediate and absolute dependence upon him [p. 232], and to quicken them if to watchfulness and prayer" (p. 227). He goes on to suggest that another design of temptation is "for the manifestation of his power, and wisdom, and grace, in supporting the soul under such pressures as are evidently beyond its own strength to sustain" (p. 228). He gives Job as an illustration. "The experiment answered many good purposes: Job was humbled, yet approved; his friends were instructed; Satan was confuted, and disappointed; and the wisdom and mercy of the Lord, in his darkest dispensations toward his people, were gloriously illustrated" (p. 228). "If the Lord has any children who are not exercised with spiritual temptations, I am sure they are but poorly qualified to 'speak a word in season to them that are weary'" (p. 231).

derful indeed! The more thou hast exalted me, the more I ought to abase myself."[73] He wrote his own epitaph:

> JOHN NEWTON,
> Clerk,
> Once an Infidel and Libertine,
> A Servant of Slaves in Africa,
> Was,
> by the rich mercy of our Lord and Savior
> JESUS CHRIST,
> Preserved, restored, pardoned,
> And appointed to preach the Faith
> He had long laboured to destroy.
> He ministered
> Near 16 years as curate and vicar
> of Olney in Bucks,
> And 28
> as rector of these united parishes.

When he wrote his *Narrative* in the early 1760s he said, "I know not that I have ever since met so daring a blasphemer."[74] The hymn we know as "Amazing Grace" was written to accompany a New Year's sermon based on 1 Chronicles 17:16, "Then King David went in and sat before the LORD, and said, 'Who am I, O LORD God, and what is my house, that you have brought me thus far?'"[75]

> *Amazing grace!—how sweet the sound—*
> *That saved a wretch like me,*
> *I once was lost, but now am found,*
> *Was blind, but now I see.*

---

[73] Cecil, *Memoirs of the Rev. John Newton*, p. 86.
[74] Ibid., p. 22.
[75] Cecil, *The Life of John Newton*, pp. 365-368.

The effect of this amazement is tenderness toward others. "[The 'wretch' who has been saved by grace] believes and feels his own weakness and unworthiness, and lives upon the grace and pardoning love of his Lord. This gives him an habitual tenderness and gentleness of spirit. Humble under a sense of much forgiveness to himself, he finds it easy to forgive others."[76]

He puts it in a picture:

A company of travelers fall into a pit: one of them gets a passenger to draw him out. Now he should not be angry with the rest for falling in; nor because they are not yet out, as he is. He did not pull himself out: instead, therefore, of reproaching them, he should show them pity. . . . A man, truly illuminated, will no more despise others, than Bartimaeus, after his own eyes were opened, would take a stick, and beat every blind man he met.[77]

Glad-hearted, grateful lowliness and brokenness as a saved "wretch" was probably the most prominent root of Newton's habitual tenderness with people.

Peaceful Confidence in the Pervasive, Loving Providence of God

In order to maintain love and tenderness that thinks more about the other person's need than our own comforts, we must have an unshakable hope that the sadness of our lives will work for our everlasting good. Otherwise we will give in, turn a deaf ear to need, and say, "Let us eat, drink, and be merry, for

---

[76] *The Works of the Rev. John Newton*, Vol. 1, p. 170.
[77] Cecil, *Memoirs of the Rev. John Newton*, p. 105.

tomorrow we die." Newton found this peace and confidence in the all-governing providence of God over good and evil. He describes his own experience when he describes the believer:

> And his faith upholds him under all trials, by assuring him that every dispensation is under the direction of his Lord; that chastisements are a token of his love; that the season, measure, and continuance of his sufferings, are appointed by Infinite Wisdom, and designed to work for his everlasting good; and that grace and strength shall be afforded him, according to his day.[78]

This keeps him from being overwhelmed with anger and bitterness and resentment when he is assaulted with pressures and disappointments. It is as practical as pastoral interruptions. "When I hear a knock at my study door, I hear a message from God. It may be a lesson of instruction; perhaps a lesson of patience: but, since it is *his* message, it must be interesting."[79] He knew that even his temptations were ordered by the sovereign goodness of God and that not to have any was dangerous for the soul. He approved of Samuel Rutherford's comment that "there is no temptation like being without temptation."[80]

And this same faith in God's gracious providence to help him profit from the painful things in life also spared him from the pleasant things in life that would deceive him and choke off the superior pleasures he has in God. If the world triumphs in this way, we will lose our joy in Christ and his mercy, and that will be the end of all Christ-exalting tenderness. So it is a crucial root

[78] *The Works of the Rev. John Newton*, Vol. 1, p. 169.
[79] Cecil, *Memoirs of the Rev. John Newton*, p. 76.
[80] *The Works of the Rev. John Newton*, Vol. 1, p. 259.

of his habitual tenderness when he says, "By faith [the believer] triumphs over [the world's] smiles and enticements: he sees that all that is in the world, suited to gratify the desires of the flesh or the eye, is not only to be avoided as sinful, but as incompatible with his best pleasures."[81]

John Newton's habitual tenderness is rooted in the sober realism of the limits of redemption in this fallen world where we "groan inwardly as we wait eagerly for . . . the redemption of our bodies" (Romans 8:23), the all-pervasive humility and gratitude for having been a blasphemer of the Gospel and now being a heaven-bound preacher of it, and the unshakable confidence that the all-governing providence of God will make every experience turn for his good, so that he doesn't spend his life murmuring, "My carriage is broken, my carriage is broken," but sings, "'Tis grace has brought me safe thus far, and grace will lead me home."

---

[81] Ibid., pp. 171-172.

My dear brother,
we must not mind a little suffering
for Christ's sake.
CHARLES SIMEON

I have continually had such a sense of my sinfulness
as would sink me into utter despair,
if I had not an assured view of the sufficiency
and willingness of Christ to save me to the uttermost.
And at the same time I had such a sense of my acceptance through
Christ as would overset my little bark, if I had not ballast at the
bottom sufficient to sink a vessel of no ordinary size.
CHARLES SIMEON

A nominal Christian is content with proving
the way of salvation by a crucified Redeemer.
But the true Christian loves it, delights in it, glories in it,
and shudders at the very thought of glorying in anything else. . . .
Let all your joys flow from the contemplation of his cross.
CHARLES SIMEON

2

CHARLES SIMEON

*The Ballast of Humiliation and
the Sails of Adoration*

In April 1831, Charles Simeon was seventy-one years old. He had been the pastor of Trinity Church in Cambridge, England, for forty-nine years. One afternoon his friend Joseph Gurney asked him how he had surmounted persecution and outlasted all the great prejudice against him in his many years of ministry. He said to Gurney:

> My dear brother, we must not mind a little suffering for Christ's sake. When I am getting through a hedge, if my head and shoulders are safely through, I can bear the pricking of my legs. Let us rejoice in the remembrance that our holy Head has surmounted all His suffering and triumphed over death. Let us follow Him patiently; we shall soon be partakers of His victory.[1]

When I set myself to meditate on the life of Charles Simeon, that is the achievement I wanted to understand. I had heard that he stayed in the same church as pastor for fifty-four years and that

---

[1] H. C. G. Moule, *Charles Simeon* (London: InterVarsity, 1948), pp. 155-156.

in the first twelve there was so much opposition from his congregation that "pewholders" locked their pews, stayed away, and forced him to preach to a standing congregation who fit in the building where they could. I wanted to verify this and understand how a man endures that kind of opposition without giving up and leaving for a more cordial reception elsewhere. My aim was to grow, and help others grow, in the biblical experience of James 1:2-3: "Count it all joy, my brothers, when you meet trials of various kinds, for you know that the testing of your faith produces steadfastness."[2]

Patience in Tribulation

So I confess at the outset that I have a spiritual and pastoral aim in this chapter, as in the whole book. I want to encourage you—as I pursue this myself—to receive and obey Romans 12:12, "Be patient in tribulation." May Simeon's life and ministry help us see persecution, opposition, slander, misunderstanding, disappointment, self-recrimination, weakness, and danger as the normal portion of faithful Christian living and ministry. I want us to see a beleaguered triumph in the life of a man who was a sinner like us and who, year after year, in his trials, "grew downward" in humility and upward in his adoration of Christ and who did not yield to bitterness or to the temptation to leave his charge—for fifty-four years.

---

[2] The Greek word translated "steadfastness" is ὑπομονήν (hupomonēn) and means "patient endurance, perseverance, steadfastness." It is clearly one of the great gifts and goals of the Christian life, as numerous texts show. Romans 2:7; 5:3; Colossians 1:11; 1 Timothy 6:11; James 5:11; 2 Peter 1:6; Revelation 2:2-3, 19.

Escaping Emotional Fragility

What I have found is that in my pastoral disappointments and discouragements there is a great power for perseverance in keeping before me the life of a person who surmounted great obstacles in obedience to God's call by the power of God's grace. I need this inspiration from another century, because I know that I am, in great measure, a child of my times. And one of the pervasive marks of our times is emotional fragility. It hangs in the air we breathe. We are easily hurt. We pout and mope easily. We blame easily. We break easily. Our marriages break easily. Our faith breaks easily. Our happiness breaks easily. And our commitment to the church breaks easily. We are easily disheartened, and it seems we have little capacity for surviving and thriving in the face of criticism and opposition.

A typical emotional response to trouble in the church is to think, *If that's the way they feel about me, then I'll just find another church.* We see very few healthy, happy examples today whose lives spell out in flesh and blood the rugged words, "Count it all joy, my brothers, when you meet trials of various kinds" (James 1:2). When historians list the character traits of America in the last third of the twentieth century, commitment, constancy, tenacity, endurance, patience, resolve, and perseverance will not be on the list. The list will begin with an all-consuming interest in self-esteem. It will be followed by the subheadings of self-assertiveness, self-enhancement, and self-realization. And if we think that we are not children of our times, let us simply test ourselves to see how we respond when people reject our ideas or spurn our good efforts or misconstrue our best intentions.

We all need help here. We are surrounded by, and are part

of, a society of emotionally fragile quitters. The spirit of the age is too much in us. We need to spend time with the kind of people—whether dead or alive—whose lives prove there is another way to live. Scripture says, be "imitators of those who through faith and *patience* inherit the promises" (Hebrews 6:12). So I want to hold up for us the faith and the patient endurance of Charles Simeon for our inspiration and imitation.

Simeon's Life and Times

Let's orient ourselves with some facts about his life and times. When Simeon was born on September 24, 1759, Jonathan Edwards had died just the year before. John and Charles Wesley and George Whitefield were still alive, and the "Methodist" awakening was in full swing. Simeon would live for seventy-seven years, from 1759 to 1836—through the American Revolution, the French Revolution, and not quite into the decade of the telegraph and the railroad.

His father was a wealthy attorney, but no believer. We know nothing of his mother. She probably died early, so that he never knew her. At seven he went to England's premier boarding school, the Royal College of Eton. He was there for twelve years and was known as a homely, fancy-dressing, athletic show-off. The atmosphere was irreligious and degenerate in many ways. Looking back late in life, he said that he would be tempted to take the life of his son rather than let him see the vice he himself had seen at Eton.[3]

He said he only knew one religious book besides the Bible in those twelve years—namely, *The Whole Duty of Man*, a devotional

---

[3] Moule, *Charles Simeon*, p. 18.

book of the seventeenth century. Whitefield thought the book so bad that once, when he caught an orphan in Georgia with a copy of it, he made him throw it in the fire. William Cowper said it was a "repository of self-righteous and pharisaical lumber."[4] That, in fact, would be a good description of Simeon's life to that point.

How God Saved Him

At nineteen he went to King's College in the University of Cambridge. In the first four months God brought him from darkness to light. The amazing thing about his conversion to Christ is that God did it against the remarkable odds of having no other Christian around. Cambridge was so destitute of evangelical faith that, even after he was converted, Simeon did not meet another believer on campus for almost three years. "The waves of the great Methodist revival appear to have left Cambridge almost or quite untouched."[5]

Three days after he arrived at Cambridge on January 29, 1779, the Provost, William Cooke, announced that Simeon had to attend the Lord's Supper. Simeon was terrified. We can see, in retrospect, that this was the work of God in his life. He knew enough to fear that it was very dangerous to eat the Lord's Supper as an unbeliever or a hypocrite. So he began desperately to read and to try to repent and make himself better. He began with *The Whole Duty of Man* but got no help. He passed through that first Communion unchanged. But he knew it wasn't the last. He turned to a book by a Bishop Wilson on the Lord's Supper. As Easter Sunday approached, a wonderful thing happened.

---

[4] R. Southey, *The Life of William Cowper* (1854), I, 81, cited in Hugh Evan Hopkins, *Charles Simeon of Cambridge* (Grand Rapids, MI: Eerdmans, 1977), p. 27.
[5] Moule, *Charles Simeon*, p. 21.

Keep in mind that this young man had almost no preparation of the kind we count so important. He had no mother to nurture him. His father was an unbeliever. His boarding school was a godless and corrupt place. And his university was destitute, as far as he knew, of other evangelical believers. He was nineteen years old, sitting in his dormitory room as Passion Week began at the end of March 1779.

Here is his own account of what happened.

> In Passion Week, as I was reading Bishop Wilson on the Lord's Supper, I met with an expression to this effect— "That the Jews knew what they did, when they transferred their sin to the head of their offering." The thought came into my mind, What, may I transfer all my guilt to another? Has God provided an Offering for me, that I may lay my sins on His head? Then, God willing, I will not bear them on my own soul one moment longer. Accordingly I sought to lay my sins upon the sacred head of Jesus; and on the Wednesday began to have a hope of mercy; on the Thursday that hope increased; on the Friday and Saturday it became more strong; and on the Sunday morning, Easter-day, April 4, I awoke early with those words upon my heart and lips, "Jesus Christ is risen to-day! Hallelujah! Hallelujah!" From that hour peace flowed in rich abundance into my soul; and at the Lord's Table in our Chapel I had the sweetest access to God through my blessed Savior.[6]

Bearing Fruit Worthy of Repentance

The effect was immediate and dramatic. His well-known extravagance gave way to a life of simplicity. This is the very same

---

[6] Ibid., pp. 25-26

effect we will see in the twenty-six-year-old William Wilberforce in the next chapter. All the rest of his life, Simeon lived in simple rooms on the university campus, moving only once to larger quarters so that he could have more students for his conversation gatherings. When his brother left him a fortune, he turned it down and channeled all his extra income to religious and charitable goals. He began at once to teach his new biblical faith to his servant girl at the college. When he went home for holidays, he called the family together for devotions. His father never came, but his two brothers were both eventually converted. And in his private life he began to practice what in those days was known as "methodism"—strict discipline in prayer and meditation.

We can catch a glimpse of his zeal from this anecdote about his early rising for Bible study and prayer.

> Early rising did not appeal to his natural tendency to self-indulgence, however, especially on dark winter mornings. . . . On several occasions he overslept, to his considerable chagrin. So he determined that if ever he did it again, he would pay a fine of half a crown to his "bed-maker" (college servant). A few days later, as he lay comfortably in his warm bed, he found himself reflecting that the good woman was poor and could probably do with half a crown. So, to overcome such rationalizations, he vowed that next time he would throw a guinea[7] into the river. This (the story goes) he duly did, but only once, for guineas were scarce; he could not afford to use them to pave the river bed with gold.[8]

---

[7] A "guinea" was a gold coin issued in England from 1663 to 1813 and worth one pound and one shilling.
[8] Ibid., p. 66.

In spite of this disciplined approach to spiritual growth, Simeon's native pride and impetuousness did not disappear overnight. We will see shortly that this was one of the thorns he would be plucking at for some time.

The Call to Trinity Church, Cambridge

After three years, in January 1782, Simeon received a fellowship at the university. This gave him a stipend and certain rights in the university. For example, over the next fifty years he was three times dean for a total of nine years, and once vice provost. But that was not his main calling. In May that year, he was ordained a deacon in the Anglican Church, and after a summer preaching interim in St. Edward's Church in Cambridge he was called to Trinity Church as vicar (pastor). He preached his first sermon there on November 10, 1782. And there he stayed for fifty-four years until his death on November 13, 1836.

Celibacy

Simeon never married. I have read only one sentence about this fact. H. C. G. Moule said he "had deliberately and resolutely chosen the then necessary celibacy of a Fellowship that he might the better work for God at Cambridge."[9] This too requires a special kind of endurance. Not many have it, and it is a beautiful thing when one finds it. Who knows how many men and women Simeon inspired with the possibility of celibacy and chastity because of his lifelong commitment to Christ and his church as an unmarried

---

[9] Ibid., p. 111.

man. One such person in our day who counts Simeon as a hero in this and other regards is John Stott, a kind of latter-day Simeon in more ways than most realize. Not only did neither marry, but both were evangelical and Anglican, Cambridge graduates, long-time pastors in one church, celibate, committed to social concern, and engaged in world evangelization.[10]

A Long Global Impact

In his fifty-four years at Trinity Church, Simeon became a powerful force for evangelicalism in the Anglican church. His position at the university, with his constant influence on students preparing for the ministry, made him a great recruiter of young evangelicals for pulpits around the land. But not only around the land. He became the trusted adviser of the East India Company and recommended most of the men who went out as chaplains, which is the way Anglicans could be missionaries to the East in those days.

Simeon had a great heart for missions. He was the spiritual father and mentor of the great Henry Martyn, who when he died in 1813 at the age of thirty-one, had been a chaplain in the

---

[10] Stott's great admiration for Simeon is unconcealed. He wrote the introduction for a collection of Simeon's sermons, *Evangelical Preaching: An Anthology of Sermons by Charles Simeon* (Sisters, OR: Multnomah Press, 1986), and confessed to a friend, "Charles Simeon of Cambridge remains something of a guru to me." Timothy Dudley-Smith, *John Stott: A Global Ministry, A Biography, the Latter Years* (Downers Grove, IL: InterVarsity Press, 2001), p. 428. The author of that biography says, "The parallels between the two men are certainly striking. Both were privileged sons of comparatively affluent parents, educated at public schools, undergraduates at Cambridge. They shared a transforming experience of conversion to Christ, early and severe trials and testing, and virtually a lifetime's ministry in a single church. Each cultivated habits well beyond the norm for early rising, disciplined prayer and the study of Scripture. Each became a mentor to students, and a leader to younger clergy as well as among his contemporaries. They shared a call to the single life, and to the rediscovery (and subsequent teaching) of the art of expository preaching. Like John Stott, Simeon had a world vision (as one of the founders of the Church Missionary Society) and a grasp of strategic organization, as in the patronage trust which he founded and which still bears his name. Each was a believer in the power of the printed word, and published many volumes of Bible exposition" (ibid., pp. 428-429).

East India Company and had in less than five years translated the New Testament into Urdu (then called Hindoostani) and Persian and supervised its translation into Arabic. Simeon was the key spiritual influence in the founding of the Church Missionary Society and was zealous in his labors for the British and Foreign Bible Society and the Society for Promoting Christianity among the Jews.[11] In fact, on his deathbed he was dictating a message to be given to the Society about his deep humiliation that the church had not done more to gather in the Jewish people.

A Preacher Without Labels

Simeon probably exerted his greatest influence through sustained biblical preaching year after year. This was the central labor of his life. He lived long enough to place into the hands of King William IV in 1833 the completed twenty-one volumes of his collected sermons. This is the best place to go to research Simeon's theology. One can find his views on almost every key text in the Bible. That is what he wanted to be above all theological labels, biblical.

He did not want to be labeled a Calvinist or an Arminian. He wanted to be faithful to Scripture through and through and give every text its due proportion, whether it sounded Arminian or Calvinistic. But he was known as an evangelical Calvinist, and rightly so. As I have read portions of his sermons on texts concerning election, effectual calling, and perseverance, I have found him uninhibited in his affirmation of what the Puritans called "the

---

[11] See the website of the Henry Martyn Center, www.martynmission.cam.ac.uk/CLife.htm.

doctrines of grace." In fact, he uses that phrase approvingly in his sermon on Romans 9:19-24.[12]

But he had little sympathy for uncharitable Calvinists. In a sermon on Romans 9:16 he said:

> Many there are who cannot see these truths [the doctrines of God's sovereignty], who yet are in a state truly pleasing to God; yea many, at whose feet the best of us may be glad to be found in heaven. It is a great evil, when these doctrines are made a ground of separation one from another, and when the advocates of different systems anathematize each other. . . . In reference to truths which are involved in so much obscurity as those which relate to the sovereignty of God, mutual kindness and concession are far better than vehement argumentation and uncharitable discussion.[13]

A Conversation with John Wesley

An example of how he lived out this counsel is seen in the way he conversed with the elderly John Wesley. He tells the story himself:

> Sir, I understand that you are called an Arminian; and I have been sometimes called a Calvinist; and therefore I suppose we are to draw daggers. But before I consent to begin the combat, with your permission I will ask you a few questions. Pray, Sir, do you feel yourself a depraved creature, so depraved that you would never have thought of turning to God, if God had not first put it into your heart?
>
> Yes, I do indeed.

---

[12] Charles Simeon, *Horae Homileticae*, Vol. 15, p. 358.
[13] Ibid., p. 357.

And do you utterly despair of recommending yourself to God by anything you can do; and look for salvation solely through the blood and righteousness of Christ?

Yes, solely through Christ.

But, Sir, supposing you were at first saved by Christ, are you not somehow or other to save yourself afterwards by your own works?

No, I must be saved by Christ from first to last.

Allowing, then, that you were first turned by the grace of God, are you not in some way or other to keep yourself by your own power?

No.

What then, are you to be upheld every hour and every moment by God, as much as an infant in its mother's arms?

Yes, altogether.

And is all your hope in the grace and mercy of God to preserve you unto His heavenly kingdom?

Yes, I have no hope but in Him.

Then, Sir, with your leave I will put up my dagger again; for this is all my Calvinism; this is my election, my justification by faith, my final perseverance: it is in substance all that I hold, and as I hold it; and therefore, if you please, instead of searching out terms and phrases to be a ground of contention between us, we will cordially unite in those things wherein we agree.[14]

But don't take this to mean that Simeon pulled any punches when expounding biblical texts. He was very forthright in teaching what the Bible teaches and calling error by its real name. But he was jealous of not getting things out of balance.

---

[14] Moule, *Charles Simeon*, pp. 79-80.

Christ, the Center of All Subjects

Hugh Evan Hopkins, a biographer of Simeon, explains the essence of his preaching:

> His matter was never trivial, and he never for a moment wandered into idle rhetoric. To expound the Scripture before him as closely and clearly as he could, and then to bring its message to bear full on the conscience and will of the hearers, was his settled aim from the first, kept in view intelligently with great pains. And what was his doctrine? In two words, it was Jesus Christ. Everything in Simeon's preaching radiated from Jesus Christ, and returned upon Him. Not that he forced texts away from their surroundings, and forgot the literal in the mystical. But he was sure that Christ is the burden of the words of the Prophets and the Apostles; and he knew that He was everything for Charles Simeon. . . . For him Christ was the centre of all subjects for sinful man; and all his hearers were for him sinful men, for whom the Gospel was the one remedy. Christ was the Gospel; and personal faith in Him, a living Person, was the Gospel secret. . . . Simeon himself thus describes the three great aims of all his preaching: *"To humble the sinner, To exalt the Saviour, To promote holiness."* [15]

Let the Bible Speak

He said that his invariable rule was "to endeavor to give to every portion of the Word of God its full and proper force, without considering what scheme it favors, or whose system it is likely to advance." [16] "My endeavor is to bring out of Scripture what is

---

[15] Ibid., p. 52.
[16] Ibid., p. 79.

there, and not to thrust in what I think might be there. I have a great jealousy on this head; never to speak more or less than I believe to be the mind of the Spirit in the passage I am expounding."[17]

He makes an observation that is true enough to sting every person who has ever been tempted to adjust Scripture to fit a system.

> Of this he [speaking of himself in the third person] is sure, that there is not a decided Calvinist or Arminian in the world who equally approves of the whole of Scripture . . . who, if he had been in the company of St. Paul whilst he was writing his Epistles, would not have recommended him to alter one or other of his expressions.
>
> But the author would not wish one of them altered; he finds as much satisfaction in one class of passages as another; and employs the one, he believes, as freely as the other. Where the inspired Writers speak in unqualified terms, he thinks himself at liberty to do the same; judging that they needed no instruction from *him* how to propagate the truth. He is content to sit as a learner at the feet of the holy Apostles and has no ambition to teach them how they ought to have spoken.[18]

With that remarkable devotion to Scripture, Simeon preached in the same pulpit for fifty-four years with a global impact. It was this combination of deep and fruitful devotion to Scripture and fifty-four years of endurance in one place of ministry, in spite of opposition and difficulty, that drew me to Simeon. That is what I turn to now. First his trials, and then finally the roots of his endurance that enabled him to press on to the end and not give up. How was he able to be so "patient in tribulation"?

---

[17] Ibid., p. 77.
[18] Ibid., p. 79.

The Unripe Self

The most fundamental trial that Simeon had—and that we all have—was himself. He had a somewhat harsh and self-assertive air about him. One day, early in Simeon's ministry, he was visiting Henry Venn, who was pastor twelve miles from Cambridge at Yelling. When he left to go home, Venn's daughters complained to their father about his manner. Venn took the girls to the backyard and said, "Pick me one of those peaches." But it was early summer, and "the time of peaches was not yet." They asked why he would want the green, unripe fruit. Venn replied, "Well, my dears, it is green now, and we must wait; but a little more sun, and a few more showers, and the peach will be ripe and sweet. So it is with Mr. Simeon."[19]

Simeon came to know himself and his sin very deeply. He described his maturing in the ministry as a growing downward. We will come back to this as the key to his great perseverance and success.

The Unwanted Vicar

The previous vicar of Trinity Church died in October 1782, just as Charles Simeon was about to leave the university to live in his father's home. Simeon had often walked by the church, he tells us, and said to himself, "How should I rejoice if God were to give me that church, that I might preach the Gospel there and be a herald for Him in the University."[20] His dream came true when Bishop Yorke appointed him "curate-in-charge" (being only

---

[19] Ibid., p. 44.
[20] Ibid., p. 37.

ordained a deacon at the time). His wealthy father had nudged the Bishop to prefer his son; and the pastor at St. Edward's, where Simeon preached that summer, gave him an endorsement. So he received the assignment and preached his first sermon at Trinity Church on November 10, 1782.

But the parishioners did not want Simeon. They wanted the assistant curate Mr. Hammond. Simeon was willing to step out, but then the Bishop told him that even if he did decline the appointment, Hammond would not be appointed. So Simeon stayed—for fifty-four years! And gradually—very gradually—overcame the opposition.

The first thing the congregation did in rebellion against Simeon was to refuse to let him be the Sunday afternoon lecturer. This second Sunday service was in their charge. For five years they assigned the lecture to Mr. Hammond. Then when he left, instead of turning it over to their pastor of five years, they gave it to another independent man for seven more years! Finally, in 1794, Simeon was chosen lecturer.[21] Thus for twelve years he served a church who was so resistant to his leadership they would not let him preach Sunday afternoons but hired an assistant to keep him out.

Simeon tried to start a later Sunday evening service, and many townspeople came. But the churchwardens locked the doors while the people stood waiting in the street. Once Simeon had the doors opened by a locksmith, but when it happened again he relented and dropped the service.

The second thing the church did was to lock the pew doors on Sunday mornings. The pewholders refused to come and refused to let others sit in their personal pews. Simeon set up seats in the

---

[21] Ibid., p. 39.

aisles and nooks and corners at his own expense. But the churchwardens took them out and threw them into the churchyard.
When he tried to visit from house to house, hardly a door would
open to him. This situation lasted at least ten years. The records
show that in 1792 Simeon got a legal decision that the pewholders could not lock their pews.[22] But he didn't use it. He let his
steady, relentless ministry of the Word and prayer and community witness gradually overcome the resistance.

But I mustn't give the impression that all the troubles were finished after the first twelve years. There were, to be sure, years of
peace, but in 1812 (after he had been there thirty years!) there
were again opponents in the congregation making the waters
rough. He wrote to a friend, "I used to sail in the Pacific; I am now
learning to navigate the Red Sea that is full of shoals and rocks."
Who of us would not have concluded that at age fifty-three, after
thirty years in one church, an upsurge of opposition is surely a sign
to move on? But again he endured patiently, and in 1815 he writes
that peace had come to the church and that he had "the joy of
ministering to an united and affectionate flock."[23]

Despised in His Own University

As the students made their way to Trinity Church, they were
prejudiced against the pastor by the hostile congregation, and
for years he was smeared with all kinds of rumors. "From the very
first, and for many years after, he was personally slandered as a
bad man who had a high profession of goodness; a terrible

---

[22] Ibid., p. 45.
[23] William Carus, *Memoirs of the Life of the Rev. Charles Simeon* (London: 1847), p. 245.

dagger-thrust at any time, but never more so than when, as then, the outward practice of religion has fallen into general neglect."[24] The students at Cambridge held Simeon in derision for his biblical preaching and his uncompromising stand as an evangelical.

They repeatedly disrupted his services and caused a carousing in the streets. One observer wrote from personal experience, "For many years Trinity Church and the streets leading to it were the scenes of the most disgraceful tumults."[25] Simeon himself tells of "several occasions [when] stones were thrown in at the windows."[26] On one occasion a band of undergraduates determined to assault Simeon personally as he left the church after service. They waited by the usual exit for him, but providentially he took another way home that day.[27] Students who were converted and wakened by Simeon's preaching were soon ostracized and ridiculed. They were called "Sims"—a term that lasted all the way to the 1860s— and their way of thinking was called derisively "Simeonism."

But harder to bear than the insults of the students was the ostracism and coldness of his peers in the university. One of the Fellows scheduled Greek classes on Sunday night to prevent students from going to Simeon's service. In another instance, one of the students who looked up to Simeon was denied an academic prize because of his "Simeonism."[28] Sometimes Simeon felt utterly alone at the university where he lived. He looked back on those early years and wrote, "I remember the time that I was quite surprised that a Fellow of my own College ventured to walk with me for a quarter of an hour on the grass-plot before Clare Hall; and for many years

---

[24] Moule, *Charles Simeon*, p. 53.
[25] Ibid., p. 58.
[26] Ibid., p. 56.
[27] Ibid., p. 59.
[28] Ibid., p. 55.

after I began my ministry I was 'as a man wondered at,' by reason of the paucity of those who showed any regard for true religion."[29]

Even after he had won the respect of many, there could be grave mistreatment. For example, even as late as 1816 (thirty-four years into his ministry) he wrote to a missionary friend, "Such conduct is observed towards me at this very hour by one of the Fellows of the College as, if practiced by *me*, would set not the College only but the whole town and University in a flame."[30]

Broken and Restored for Ministry in Old Age

In 1807, after twenty-five years of ministry, his health failed suddenly. His voice gave way so that preaching was very difficult and at times he could only speak in a whisper. After a sermon he would feel "more like one dead than alive."[31] This broken condition lasted for thirteen years, till he was sixty years old. In all this time Simeon pressed on in his work.

The way this weakness came to an end is remarkable and shows the amazing hand of God on Simeon's life. "It passed away quite suddenly and without any evident physical cause."[32] He tells the story that in 1819 he was on his last visit to Scotland. As he crossed the border he says he was "almost as perceptibly revived in strength as the woman was after she had touched the hem of our Lord's garment."[33] His interpretation of God's providence in this begins back before the weakness had befallen him in 1807. Up till then he had promised himself a very active life

---

[29] Ibid., p. 59.
[30] Ibid., p. 127.
[31] Ibid., p. 125.
[32] Ibid.
[33] Ibid.

up to age sixty, and then a Sabbath evening. Now he seemed to
hear his Master saying:

> I laid you aside, because you entertained with satisfaction
> the thought of resting from your labor; but now you have
> arrived at the very period when you had promised yourself
> that satisfaction, and have determined instead to spend
> your strength for me to the latest hour of your life, I have
> doubled, trebled, quadrupled your strength, that you may
> execute your desire on a more extended plan.[34]

So at sixty years of age, Simeon renewed his commitment to
his pulpit and the local and global mission of the church and
preached vigorously for seventeen more years, until two months
before his death. Surely there is a lesson for us here concerning
retirement. Is there any biblical warrant for the modern, western assumption that old age or retirement years are to be years
of coasting or easing up or playing? I am not aware of such a
principle in the Bible. In fact, it is a great sadness to see so many
older Christians adapting to this cultural norm and wasting the
last decades of their lives in innocent lounging around. Who
knows but that greater strength and health would be given if
there were resolves to move toward need and not comfort in
our old age? Who knows whether God would give awakening
and renewal if we would renew our dreams of ministry to the perishing world and not just the "ministry" of playing with our
grandchildren?

---

[34] Ibid.

The Roots of His Endurance

How did Simeon endure his trials for so long without giving up or being driven out of his church? There were numerous biblical strategies of endurance. But there was also a root that was deeper than the particular forms and strategies of endurance. First we will look at the forms and strategies of endurance, and finally focus on the root that sustained them all.

A Strong Sense of His Accountability Before God for the Souls of His Flock

In his first year in the pulpit he preached a sermon about his accountability before God and said to the people standing in the aisles:

> Remember the nature of my office, and the care incumbent on me for the welfare of your immortal souls. . . . Consider whatever may appear in my discourses harsh, earnest or alarming, not as the effects of enthusiasm, but as the rational dictates of a heart impressed with a sense both of the value of the soul and the importance of eternity. . . . By recollecting the awful consequences of my neglect, you will be more inclined to receive favorably any well-meant admonitions.[35]

Fifteen years later he preached on the subject again. Years after this sermon, one of his friends told of how its power was still being felt. Simeon said the pastor is like the keeper of a lighthouse. He painted a vivid picture of a rocky coast strewn with dead and mangled bodies with the wailing of widows and

---

[35] Ibid., p. 46.

orphans. He pictured the delinquent keeper being brought out and at last the answer given: "Asleep!"[36] The way he made this word burst on the ears of the hearers never let at least one of them ever forget what is at stake in the pastoral ministry. Wakeful endurance was a life-and-death matter for Simeon. He dared not have a casual, sleepy-eyed approach to ministry.

It did not matter that his people were often against him. He was not commissioned by them, but by the Lord. And they were his responsibility. He believed Hebrews 13:17—that he would one day have to give an account for the souls of his church.

Free from the Scolding Tone Even Through Controversy

How many times have we heard a pastor's wounded pride or his personal anger at parishioners seeping through his preaching! This is deadly for the ministry. Moule, Simeon's biographer, said of him that his style of address in those early years of intense opposition was "totally free from that easy but fatal mistake of troubled pastors, the scolding accent."[37]

Years after his conversion he said that his security in God gave him the capacity to be hopeful in the presence of other people even when burdened within: "With this sweet hope of ultimate acceptance with God, I have always enjoyed much cheerfulness before men; but I have at the same time labored incessantly to cultivate the deepest humiliation before God."[38]

Joseph Gurney saw the same thing in Simeon for years and wrote, that in spite of Simeon's private weeping, "it was one of

---

[36] Hopkins, *Charles Simeon of Cambridge*, pp. 64-65.
[37] Moule, *Charles Simeon*, p. 46.
[38] Hopkins, *Charles Simeon of Cambridge*, p. 156.

his grand principles of action, to endeavor at all times to honor his Master by maintaining a cheerful happy demeanor in the presence of his friends."[39] He had evidently learned the lesson of Matthew 6:17-18, "But when you fast, anoint your head and wash your face, that your fasting may not be seen by others but by your Father who is in secret."

Simeon's joyful, life-giving demeanor can perhaps best be seen in the descriptions of him by William Cowper and William Wilberforce. Cowper wrote:

> *. . . with a smile*
> *Gentle and affable, and full of grace,*
> *As fearful of offending whom he wish'd*
> *Much to persuade, he plied his ear with truths*
> *Not harshly thunder'd forth or rudely press'd*
> *But, like his purpose, gracious, kind and sweet.*[40]

And Wilberforce recorded in his journal: "Simeon with us— his heart glowing with love of Christ. How full he is of love, and of desire to promote the spiritual benefit of others. Oh! that I might copy him as he Christ."[41]

Not a Rumor-Tracker

He was like Charles Spurgeon who gave a lecture to his students titled "The Blind Eye and the Deaf Ear."[42] The pastor must have

---

[39] Moule, *Charles Simeon*, p. 157.

[40] Hopkins, *Charles Simeon of Cambridge*, p. 66.

[41] Ibid., p. 166.

[42] Charles Spurgeon, *Lectures to My Students* (Grand Rapids, MI: Zondervan Publishing House, 1972), pp. 321-335.

one blind eye and one deaf ear, and turn that eye and that ear to the rumors that would incense him.

Simeon was deeply wronged in 1821. We are not given the details. But when he was asked about his response (which had evidently been non-retaliatory) he said, "My rule is—never to hear, or see, or know, what if heard, or seen, or known, would call for animadversion from me. Hence it is that I dwell in peace in the midst of lions."[43] In other words, we would all do well not to be curious about what others are saying about us. There is little good that can come of it: pride, if the comments are good; discouragement, if they are critical; anger, if they are false. These are not the emotions we need to cultivate. Trusted counsel from reliable people, not rumors, is the stuff of good self-assessment.

Not a Heresy-Hunter

A pastor wrote to Simeon, wanting him to "answer and knock down" a certain preacher whom he suspected of doctrinal error. But Simeon was more exercised by the manner in which this informing pastor sought to go about this controversy. He wrote back to him:

> I know you will forgive me if I say that the very account you give of yourself in relation to controversy is a dissuasive from embarking in it. Let a man once engage in it, and it is surprising how the love of it will grow upon him; and he will find both a hare in every bush, and will follow it with something of a huntsman's feelings.[44]

---

[43] Moule, *Charles Simeon*, p. 191.
[44] Hopkins, *Charles Simeon of Cambridge*, p. 171.

Controversy and doctrinal accountability are tasks we must engage in until the Lord returns. It is not a happy business, but it is a necessary one. And in so doing, we must all heed Simeon's words to examine our motives lest we love controversy more than the truth itself.

Dealing with Opponents in a Forthright, Face-to-Face Way

In 1810 a man named Edward Pearson accused Simeon of setting too high a standard of holiness in his preaching. This criticism was made public in pamphlets. Simeon wrote to Pearson and said:

> Persons who have the same general design, but differ in some particular modes of carrying it into execution, often stand more aloof from each other than they do from persons whose principles and conduct they entirely disapprove. Hence prejudice arises and a tendency to mutual crimination; whereas, if they occasionally conversed for half an hour with each other, they would soon rectify their mutual misapprehensions, and concur in aiding, rather than undermining, the efforts of each other for the public good.[45]

It is remarkable, as Simeon said, how much evil can be averted by doing things face to face. We attempt far too much fence mending today by letter or e-mail or phone. There is something mysteriously powerful about the peacemaking potentials of personal, face-to-face conversation. It did not spare Simeon years of criticism, but it was surely one of the means God used to overcome the opposition in the long run.

---

[45] Ibid., pp. 126-127.

Receiving Rebuke and Growing from It

Receiving and benefiting from criticism is utterly essential to survive and thrive in Christian life and ministry. We need to absorb and profit from reproof—from the Lord and from man. Recall how Simeon interpreted his thirteen-year weakness from age forty-seven to sixty as a rebuke from the Lord for his intention to retire at sixty. He took it well and gave himself with all his might to the ministry of the Word until he died. At seventy-six he wrote, "Through mercy I am, for ministerial service, stronger than I have been at any time this thirty years . . . preaching at seventy-six with all the exuberance of youth . . . but looking for my dismission [death] daily."[46] He was not embittered by a thirteen-year rebuke. He was impelled by it.

It was the same with rebukes from men. If these rebukes came from his enemies, his sentiment was the sentiment of Genesis 50:20: "As for you, you meant evil against me, but God meant it for good." Simeon said, "If I suffer with a becoming spirit, my enemies, though unwittingly, must of necessity do me good."[47]

But his friends rebuked him as well. For example, he had the bad habit of speaking as if he were very angry about mere trifles. One day at a Mr. Hankinson's house he became so irritated at how the servant was stoking the fire that he gave him a swat on the back to get him to stop. Then when he was leaving, the servant got a bridle mixed up, and Simeon's temper broke out violently against the man. Mr. Hankinson wrote a letter as if from his servant and put it in Simeon's bag to be found later. In it he said that he did not see how a man who preached and prayed so well

---

[46] Ibid., p. 162.
[47] Ibid., p. 39.

could be in such a passion about nothing and wear no *bridle* on his tongue. He signed it "John Softly."

Simeon responded (on April 12, 1804) directly to the servant with the words, "To John Softly, from Charles, Proud and Irritable: I most cordially thank you, my dear friend, for your kind and seasonable reproof." Then he wrote to his friend Mr. Hankinson, "I hope, my dearest brother, that when you find your soul nigh to God, you will remember one who so greatly needs all the help he can get."[48] We will see the root of this willingness to be humbled in just a moment.

Unimpeachable in His Finances with No Love of Money

He gave his enemies no foothold when it came to lifestyle and wealth. He lived as a single man simply in his rooms at the university and gave all his excess income to the poor of the community. He turned down the inheritance of his rich brother.[49] Moule said he had "a noble indifference to money."[50] And his active involvement with the relief for the poor in the area went a long way toward overcoming the prejudices against him. It is hard to be the enemy of a person who is full of practical good deeds. In

---

[48] Ibid., p. 147.

[49] In a memorandum Simeon wrote to explain why, with his resources, he did not abandon his role as and dependence on the modest living of a University Fellow: "My brother was extremely liberal. . . . . At his death an exceeding great void would have been made, if I had not determined to accept a part of his property and to appropriate it to the Lord's service and the service of the poor. The loss they would have sustained being about £700 or £800 a year, I suffered my brother to leave me £15,000, and have regularly consecrated the interest of it to the Lord; and shall (D.V.) continue to do so to my dying hour. Had I wished for money for my own use, I might have had half his fortune; but I wanted nothing for myself, being determined (as far as such a thing could be at any time said to be determined) to live and die in the College, where the income which I previously enjoyed (though moderate in itself) sufficed not only for all my own wants, but for liberal supplies to the poor also. . . . The fact is, I have not increased my own expenditure above £50 a year; nor do I consider myself as anything but a steward of my deceased brother for the poor." Quoted in Arthur J. Tait, *Charles Simeon and His Trust* (London: Society for Promoting Christian Knowledge, 1936), pp. 51-52.

[50] Moule, *Charles Simeon*, p. 129.

this way he put into practice the counsel of the apostle Peter: "This is the will of God, that by doing good you should put to silence the ignorance of foolish men" (1 Peter 2:15).

Seeing Discouraging Things Hopefully

When the members of his congregation locked their pews and kept them locked for over ten years, Simeon said:

> In this state of things I saw no remedy but faith and patience. The passage of Scripture which subdued and controlled my mind was this, "The servant of the Lord must not strive" [2 Timothy 2:24]. It was painful indeed to see the church, with the exception of the aisles, almost forsaken; but I thought that if God would only give a double blessing to the congregation that did attend, there would on the whole be as much good done as if the congregation were doubled and the blessing limited to only half the amount. This comforted me many, many times, when, without such a reflection, I should have sunk under my burden.[51]

One illustration of the truth of Simeon's confidence is the story of one of his preaching trips to Scotland. He happened to visit the home of a minister named Stewart who was not truly converted and was quite miserable. Through the personal life and witness of Simeon, Mr. Stewart was transformed and for fifteen years afterward was powerful for the Gospel.

One of the couples who said later that they "owed their own selves" to the new preaching of Mr. Stewart were the parents of Alexander Duff. They brought up their son in the full faith of the

---

[51] Ibid., p. 39.

Gospel and with a special sense of dedication to the service of Christ. Duff, in turn, became one of the great Scottish missionaries to India for over fifty years. So it is true that you never know when the Lord may give a double blessing on your ministry to a small number and multiply it thirty-, sixty-, or a hundredfold even after you are dead and gone. This confidence kept Simeon going more than once.

Suffering as a Privilege of Bearing the Cross with Christ

One striking witness to this was during a time when the university was especially cold and hostile to him.

> I was an object of much contempt and derision in the University. I strolled forth one day, buffeted and afflicted with my little Testament in my hand, I prayed earnestly to my God that He would comfort me with some cordial from His Word, and that, on opening the book, I might find some text which should sustain me. It was not for direction I was looking, for I am no friend to such superstitions . . . but only for support. The first text which caught my eye was this: *"They found a man of Cyrene, Simon by name; him they compelled to bear His cross."* You know Simon is the same name as Simeon. What a word of instruction was there—what a blessed hint of my encouragement! To have the cross laid upon me, that I might bear it after Jesus—what a privilege! It was enough. Now I could leap and sing for joy as one whom Jesus was honoring with a participation of His sufferings.[52]

We recall his words when he was seventy-one and Joseph Gurney asked him how he had surmounted his persecution for

---

[52] Ibid., pp. 59-60.

forty-nine years. He said, "My dear brother, we must not mind a
little suffering for Christ's sake."

The Deepest Root of Simeon's Endurance

But where now did this remarkable power and all these forms
and strategies of endurance come from? Simeon did not respond
to trial and suffering the way ordinary humans respond.
Something else was at work here than a mere man. Beneath the
forms of his endurance was a life of prayer and meditation that
drew up resources for the battle from some deeper place. Both
prayer and meditation were essential to tap the grace of God.
"Meditation is the grand means of our growth in grace; without
it, prayer itself is an empty service."[53] A friend of Simeon's named
Housman lived with him for a few months and tells us about this
discipline of prayer and the Word.

> Simeon invariably arose every morning, though it was the
> winter season, at four o'clock; and, after lighting his fire,
> he devoted the first four hours of the day to private prayer
> and the devotional study of the Scriptures. . . . Here was
> the secret of his great grace and spiritual strength. Deriving
> instruction from such a source, and seeking it with such
> diligence, he was comforted in all his trials and prepared
> for every duty.[54]

Yes, it was a secret of his strength. But it was not the deepest
secret. *What* Simeon experienced in the Word and prayer was

---

[53] Ibid., pp. 137-138.
[54] Ibid., p. 66.

extraordinary. It is so utterly different from the counsel we receive today that it is worth looking at carefully.

Growing Downward in Humiliation Before God, Upward in Adoration of Christ

Handley Moule captures the essence of Simeon's secret of longevity in this sentence: "'Before honor is humility,' and he had been *'growing downwards'* year by year under the stern discipline of difficulty met in the right way, the way of *close and adoring communion with God.*"[55] Those two things were the heartbeat of Simeon's inner life: growing downward in humility and growing upward in adoring communion with God.

But the remarkable thing about humiliation and adoration in the heart of Charles Simeon is that they were inseparable. Simeon was utterly unlike most of us today who think that we should get rid once and for all of feelings of vileness and unworthiness as soon as we can. For him, adoration only grew in the freshly plowed soil of humiliation for sin. So he actually labored to know his true sinfulness and his remaining corruption as a Christian.

> I have continually had such a sense of my sinfulness as would sink me into utter despair, if I had not an assured view of the sufficiency and willingness of Christ to save me to the uttermost. And at the same time I had such a sense of my acceptance through Christ as would overset my little bark, if I had not ballast at the bottom sufficient to sink a vessel of no ordinary size.[56]

---

[55] Ibid., p. 64.
[56] Ibid., p. 134.

The Ballast of Humiliation

He never lost sight of the need for the heavy ballast of his own humiliation. After he had been a Christian forty years he wrote:

> With this sweet hope of ultimate acceptance with God, I have always enjoyed much cheerfulness before men; but I have at the same time labored incessantly to cultivate the deepest humiliation before God. I have never thought that the circumstance of God's having forgiven me, was any reason why I should forgive myself; on the contrary, I have always judged it better to loathe myself the more, in proportion as I was assured that God was pacified towards me (Ezekiel 16:63). . . . . There are but two objects that I have ever desired for these forty years to behold; the one, is my own vileness; and the other is, the glory of God in the face of Jesus Christ: and I have always thought that they should be viewed together; just as Aaron confessed all the sins of all Israel whilst he put them on the head of the scapegoat. The disease did not keep him from applying to the remedy, nor did the remedy keep him from feeling the disease. By this I seek to be, not only *humble and thankful* but *humbled in thankfulness*, before my God and Savior continually.[57]

If Simeon is right, vast portions of contemporary Christianity are wrong. And I can't help wondering whether one of the reasons we are emotionally capsized so easily today—so vulnerable to winds of criticism or opposition—is that in the name of forgiveness and grace, we have thrown the ballast overboard. Simeon's boat drew a lot of water. But it was steady and on course and the mastheads were higher and the sails bigger and more full of the

---

[57] Carus, *Memoirs of the Life of the Rev. Charles Simeon*, pp. 303-304.

Spirit than most people's today who talk more of self-esteem than self-humbling.

Ballast Below, Full Sails Above—at the Same Time

One of Simeon's missionary friends wrote about a time in 1794 when a certain Mr. Marsden entered Simeon's room and found him "so absorbed in the contemplation of the Son of God, and so overpowered with a display of His mercy to his soul, that he was incapable of pronouncing a single word," till at length he exclaimed, "Glory, glory." Only a few days later the missionary friend found Simeon at the hour of the private lecture on Sunday scarcely able to speak, "from a deep humiliation and contrition."[58]

Moule comments that these two experiences are not the alternating excesses of an ill-balanced mind. Rather they are "the two poles of a sphere of profound experience."[59] For Simeon, adoration of God grew best in the plowed soil of his own contrition. He had no fear of turning up every sin in his life and looking upon it with great grief and hatred, because he had such a vision of Christ's sufficiency that this would always result in deeper cleansing and adoration.

Humiliation and adoration were inseparable. He wrote to Mary Elliott, the sister of the writer of the hymn "Just as I Am":

> I would have the whole of my experience one continued sense—first, of my nothingness, and dependence on God; second, of my guiltiness and desert before Him; third, of my obligations to redeeming love, as utterly overwhelming

[58] Moule, *Charles Simeon*, p. 135.
[59] Ibid.

me with its incomprehensible extent and grandeur. Now I do not see why any one of these should swallow up another.[60]

As an old man he said, "I have had deep and abundant cause for humiliation, [but] I have never ceased to wash in that fountain that was opened for sin and uncleanness, or to cast myself upon the tender mercy of my reconciled God."[61] He was convinced that biblical doctrines "at once most abase and most gladden the soul."[62] He spoke once to the Duchess de Broglie when he made a visit to the Continent. He commented later, "[I] opened to her my views of the Scripture system . . . and showed her that brokenness of heart is the key to the whole."[63]

"My Proper Place"

He actually fled for refuge to the place that many today try so hard to escape.

> Repentance is in every view so desirable, so necessary, so suited to honor God, that I seek that above all. The tender heart, the broken and contrite spirit, are to me far above all the joys that I could ever hope for in this vale of tears. I long to be in my proper place, my hand on my mouth, and my mouth in the dust. . . . I feel this to be safe ground. Here I cannot err. . . . I am sure that whatever God may despise . . . He will not despise the broken and contrite heart.[64]

---

[60] Ibid., pp. 160-161.
[61] Carus, *Memoirs of the Life of the Rev. Charles Simeon*, pp. 518-519.
[62] Moule, *Charles Simeon*, p. 67.
[63] Ibid., p. 96.
[64] Ibid., pp. 133-134.

On the occasion of the fiftieth anniversary of his work at Trinity Church, looking back over his many successes, he said, "I love the valley of humiliation. I there feel that I am in my proper place."[65]

In the last months of his life he wrote, "In truth, I love to see the creature annihilated in the apprehension, and swallowed up in God; I am then safe, happy, triumphant."[66] Why? Why is this evangelical humiliation a place of happiness for Simeon? Listen to the benefits he sees in this kind of experience:

> By constantly meditating on the goodness of God and on our great deliverance from that punishment which our sins have deserved, we are brought to feel our vileness and utter unworthiness; and while we continue in this spirit of self-degradation, everything else will go on easily. We shall find ourselves advancing in our course; we shall feel the presence of God; we shall experience His love; we shall live in the enjoyment of His favor and in the hope of His glory. . . . You often feel that your prayers scarcely reach the ceiling; but, oh, get into this humble spirit by considering how good the Lord is, and how evil you all are, and then prayer will mount on wings of faith to heaven. The sigh, the groan of a broken heart, will soon go through the ceiling up to heaven, aye, into the very bosom of God.[67]

A Focus on God, Not on Self

Simeon saw that the pathway to genuine humility could not be had by looking inward—either in thinking little of his gifts or in

---

[65] Ibid., pp. 159-160.
[66] Ibid., p. 162.
[67] Ibid., pp. 137-138.

thinking much about his sins. The key was to look away from himself and toward *God*. Hopkins writes:

> Self-humiliation for Simeon consisted not of belittling the gifts that God had given him or pretending that he was a man of no account, or exaggerating the sins of which he was very conscious. He went about it by consciously bringing himself into the presence of God, dwelling thoughtfully on his majesty and glory, magnifying the mercy of his forgiveness and the wonder of his love. These were the things that humbled him—not so much his own sinfulness but God's incredible love.[68]

All the way to the end of his life, Simeon was focused upon the centrality of God as the root of his acceptance and endurance. He found his assurance, he said, "in the *sovereignty* of God in choosing such a one—and the *mercy* of God in pardoning such a one—and the *patience* of God in bearing with such a one—and the *faithfulness* of God in perfecting his work and performing all his promises to such a one."[69]

"I Am Enjoying" . . . the Cross

My conclusion is that the secret of Charles Simeon's perseverance was that he never threw overboard the heavy ballast of his own humiliation for sin and that this helped keep his masts erect and his sails full of the spirit of adoration. "I love simplicity; I love contrition. . . . I love the religion of heaven; to fall on our faces while we adore the Lamb is the kind of religion which my soul

---

[68] Hopkins, *Charles Simeon of Cambridge*, p. 156.
[69] Ibid., p. 181.

affects."[70] He once said that "there are but two lessons for Christians to learn: the one is, to enjoy God in everything; the other is, to enjoy everything in God."[71] As he lay dying in October 1836, a friend sat by his bed and asked what he was thinking of just then. He answered, "I don't think now; I am *enjoying.*"[72]

He grew downward in the pain of contrition, and he grew upward in the joy of adoration. And the weaving together of these two experiences into one is the achievement of the cross of Christ and the root of Simeon's great endurance. He loved to contemplate the cross of Christ not only because it signified "salvation through a crucified Redeemer," but also because by this cross he had died to the pleasures, riches, and honors of this world. Man's admiration could not lure him; man's condemnation could not lame him. He was dead to all that now, because "by [the cross] the world has been crucified to me, and I to the world" (Galatians 6:14). The cross was the place of his greatest humiliation and the place of his greatest adoration. It was death-dealing and life-giving. Therefore Simeon said that he, like Paul, "would 'know nothing else' (1 Corinthians 2:2) and 'glory in nothing else' (Galatians 6:14)."[73]

Christ was crucified for him. He was crucified with Christ. This was the key to life and endurance. This was "the power of God and the wisdom of God" (1 Corinthians 1:24).

So unfathomable are the counsels of divine wisdom contained in it, that all the angels of heaven are searching into it with a thirst that is insatiable. Such is its efficacy, that nothing can withstand its influence. By this then, my

---

70 Ibid., pp. 83-84.
71 Hopkins, *Charles Simeon of Cambridge,* p. 203.
72 Moule, *Charles Simeon,* p. 172.
73 Simeon, *Evangelical Preaching: An Anthology of Sermons by Charles Simeon,* p. 68.

brethren, you may judge whether you are Christians in deed and in truth, or whether you are only such in name. . . . For a nominal Christian is content with *proving* the way of salvation by a crucified Redeemer. But the true Christian *loves* it, *delights* in it, *glories* in it, and *shudders* at the very thought of glorying in anything else.[74]

Here is the root of Simeon's endurance: the cross of Christ giving rise to a "shuddering delight"—shuddering at his own remaining corruption that may betray his soul by fear of man and the love of the world; delight that rises higher than all that man can take or give, and therefore triumphs over all threats and allurements. Christ is all. "Let all your joys flow from the contemplation of his cross."[75]

---

[74] Ibid., p. 71. Emphasis added.
[75] Ibid.

The fatal habit of considering Christian morals as distinct from Christian doctrines insensibly gained strength. Thus the peculiar doctrines of Christianity went more and more out of sight, and as might naturally have been expected, the moral system itself also began to wither and decay, being robbed of that which should have supplied it with life and nutriment.

WILLIAM WILBERFORCE

We can scarcely indeed look into any part of the sacred volume without meeting abundant proofs that it is the religion of the Affections which God particularly requires. . . . Joy . . . is enjoined on us as our bounden duty and commended to us as our acceptable worship. . . . A cold . . . unfeeling heart is represented as highly criminal.

WILLIAM WILBERFORCE

If we would . . . rejoice in [Christ] as triumphantly as the first Christians did; we must learn, like them to repose our entire trust in him and to adopt the language of the apostle, "God forbid that I should glory, save in the cross of Jesus Christ." "Who of God is made unto us wisdom and righteousness and sanctification, and redemption."

WILLIAM WILBERFORCE

His presence was as fatal to dullness as to immorality. His mirth was as irresistible as the first laughter of childhood.

JAMES STEPHEN

3

WILLIAM WILBERFORCE

*"Peculiar Doctrines," Spiritual Delight, and
the Politics of Slavery*

Against great obstacles William Wilberforce, an evangelical member of Parliament, fought for the abolition of the African slave trade and against slavery itself until they were both illegal in the British empire. The battle consumed almost forty-six years of his life (from 1787 to 1833). The defeats and setbacks along the way would have caused the ordinary politician to embrace a more popular cause. Though he never lost a parliamentary election from age twenty-one to seventy-four, the cause of abolishing the slave trade was defeated eleven times before its passage in 1807. And the battle for abolishing slavery itself did not gain the decisive victory until three days before he died in 1833. What were the roots of this man's endurance in the cause of public righteousness?

What Made Him Tick?

To understand and appreciate the life and labor of William Wilberforce, one of the wisest things to do is to read his own book, *A Practical View of Christianity*, first, and then read biographies. The book was published in 1797 when Wilberforce was thirty-seven years old and had been a member of the British

Parliament already for sixteen years. It proved incredibly popular for the time, going through five printings in six months and being translated into five foreign languages. The book makes crystal-clear what drives Wilberforce as a person and a politician. Hearing it from his own mouth, as it were, will make the reading of all the biographies more fruitful. They don't always put a premium on what he does. So it can easily be missed, if we don't read Wilberforce first.

What made Wilberforce tick was a profound biblical allegiance to what he called the "peculiar doctrines" of Christianity. These, he said, give rise in turn to true "affections" for spiritual things, which then break the power of pride and greed and fear and lead to transformed morals, which lead to the political welfare of the nation. No true Christian can endure in battling unrighteousness unless his heart is aflame with new spiritual affections, or passions. "Mere knowledge is confessedly too weak. The affections alone remain to supply the deficiency."[1] This is the key to public and political morality. "If . . . a principle of true Religion [the Spirit-given new affections] should . . . gain ground, there is no estimating the effects on public morals, and the consequent influence on our political welfare."[2]

The Great Doer

But he was no ordinary pragmatist or political utilitarian, even though he was one of the most practical men of his day. Yes, he was a great doer. One of his biographers said, "He lacked time

---

[1] William Wilberforce, *A Practical View of Christianity*, ed. Kevin Charles Belmonte (Peabody, MA: Hendrickson Publishers, 1996), p. 51.
[2] Ibid., p. 211.

for half the good works in his mind."[3] James Stephen, who knew him well, remarked, "Factories did not spring up more rapidly in Leeds and Manchester than schemes of benevolence beneath his roof."[4] "No man," Wilberforce wrote, "has a right to be idle." "Where is it," he asked, "that in such a world as this, [that] health, and leisure, and affluence may not find some ignorance to instruct, some wrong to redress, some want to supply, some misery to alleviate?"[5] In other words, he lived to do good—or as Jesus said, to let his light shine before men that they might see his good deeds and give glory to his Father in heaven (Matthew 5:16).

> There is little doubt that Wilberforce changed the moral outlook of Great Britain. . . . The reformation of manners [morals] grew into Victorian virtues and Wilberforce touched the world when he made goodness fashionable. . . . Contrast the late eighteenth century . . . with its loose morals and corrupt public life, with the mid-nineteenth century. Whatever its faults, nineteenth-century British public life became famous for its emphasis on character, morals, and justice and the British business world famous for integrity.[6]

But he was practical with a difference. He believed with all his heart that new affections for God were the key to new morals and lasting political reformation. And these new affections and this reformation did not come from mere ethical systems. They came from what he called the "peculiar doctrines" of Christianity.

---

[3] John Pollock, *Wilberforce* (London: Constable and Company, 1977), p. 223.
[4] Ibid.
[5] Wilberforce, *A Practical View of Christianity*, p. 90.
[6] John Pollock, "A Man Who Changed His Times," in Os Guinness, ed., *Character Counts: Leadership Qualities in Washington, Wilberforce, Lincoln, and Solzhenitsyn* (Grand Rapids, MI: Baker Book House, 1999), p. 87.

For Wilberforce, practical deeds were born in "peculiar doctrines." By that term he simply meant the central distinguishing doctrines of human depravity, divine judgment, the substitutionary work of Christ on the cross, justification by faith alone, regeneration by the Holy Spirit, and the practical necessity of fruit in a life devoted to good deeds.[7]

The Fatal Habit of Nominal Christians

He wrote his book to show that the "bulk"[8] of Christians in England were merely nominal because they had abandoned these doctrines in favor of a system of ethics and had thus lost the power of ethical life and the political welfare. He wrote:

> The fatal habit of considering Christian morals as distinct from Christian doctrines insensibly gained strength. Thus the peculiar doctrines of Christianity went more and more out of sight, and as might naturally have been expected, the moral system itself also began to wither and decay, being robbed of that which should have supplied it with life and nutriment.[9]

He pled with nominal Christians of England not to turn "their eyes from the grand peculiarities of Christianity, [but] to keep these ever in view, as the pregnant principles whence all the rest must derive their origin, and receive their best support."[10]

Knowing that Wilberforce was a politician all his adult life,

---

[7] "The grand radical defect in the practical system of these nominal Christians, is their forgetfulness of all the peculiar doctrines of the Religion which they profess—the corruption of human nature—the atonement of the Savior—the sanctifying influence of the Holy Spirit." Ibid., pp. 162-163.

[8] His favorite word for the majority of nominal Christians in Britain in his day.

[9] Wilberforce, *A Practical View of Christianity*, p. 198.

[10] Ibid., p. 70.

who never lost an election from the time he was twenty-one years old, we might be tempted to think that his motives were purely pragmatic—as if he should say, "If Christianity works to pro- duce the political welfare, then use it." But that is not the spirit of his mind or his life. In fact, he believed that such pragmatism would ruin the very thing it sought, the reformation of culture.

The Decisive Direction of Sin: Vertical

Take the example of how people define sin. When considering the nature of sin, Wilberforce said, the vast bulk of Christians in England estimated the guilt of an action "not by the proportion in which, according to scripture, [actions] are offensive to God, but by that in which they are injurious to society."[11] Now, on the face of it that sounds noble, loving, and practical. Sin hurts peo- ple, so don't sin.

Wouldn't that definition of sin be good for society? But Wilberforce says, "Their slight notions of the guilt and evil of sin [reveal] an utter [lack] of all suitable reverence for the Divine Majesty. This principle [reverence for the Divine Majesty] is justly termed in Scripture, 'The beginning of wisdom' [Psalm 111:10]."[12] And without this wisdom, there will be no deep and lasting good done for man, spiritually or politically. Therefore, the supremacy of God's glory in all things is what he calls "the grand governing maxim" in all of life.[13] The good of society may never be put ahead of this. That would dishonor God and, paradoxically, defeat the

---

[11] Ibid., p. 147.
[12] Ibid., p. 149.
[13] Ibid., p. 81.

good of society. For the good of society, the good of society must not be the primary good.

What's Wrong with Dueling?

A practical example of how his mind worked is shown in his approach to the practice of dueling. Wilberforce hated this folly—the practice that demanded that a man of honor accept a challenge to a duel when another felt insulted. Wilberforce's close friend, the Prime Minister William Pitt, actually fought a duel with George Tierney in 1798, and Wilberforce was shocked that the Prime Minister would risk his life and the nation in this way.[14] Many opposed it on its human unreasonableness. But Wilberforce wrote:

> It seems hardly to have been noticed in what chiefly consists its *essential* guilt; that it is a deliberate preference of the favor of man, before the favor and approbation of God, *in articulo mortis* ["at the point of death"], in an instance, wherein our own life, and that of a fellow creature are at stake, and wherein we run the risk of rushing into the presence of our Maker in the very act of offending him.[15]

In other words, offending God is the essential consideration, not killing a man or imperiling a nation. That is what made Wilberforce tick. He was not a political pragmatist. He was a radically God-centered Christian who was a politician. And his

---

[14] Pollock, *Wilberforce*, p. 162.
[15] Wilberforce, *A Practical View of Christianity*, pp. 115-116.

true affections for God based on the "peculiar doctrines" of Christianity were the roots of his endurance in the cause of justice.

His Early Life

Wilberforce was born August 24, 1759, in Hull, England. His father died just before Wilberforce turned nine years old. He was sent to live with his uncle and aunt, William and Hannah, where he came under evangelical influences. His mother was more high church and was concerned her son was "turning Methodist." So she took him out of the boarding school where they had sent him and put him in another.[16] He had admired George Whitefield, John Wesley, and John Newton as a child. But soon he left all the influence of the evangelicals behind. At his new school, he said later, "I did nothing at all." That lifestyle continued through his years in St. John's College at Cambridge. He was able to live off his parents' wealth and get by with little work. He lost any interest in biblical religion and loved circulating among the social elite.

He became friends with his contemporary, William Pitt, who in just a few years, at the age of twenty-four in 1783, became the Prime Minister of England. On a lark, Wilberforce stood for the seat in the House of Commons for his hometown of Hull in 1780 when he was twenty-one. He spent £8,000 on the election. The money and his incredible gift for speaking triumphed over both his opponents. Pitt said Wilberforce possessed "the greatest natural eloquence of all the men I ever knew."[17] Wilberforce never lost an election during his lifelong political career.

---

[16] Pollock, *Wilberforce*, p. 5.
[17] Pollock, "A Man Who Changed His Times," p. 78.

Thus began a fifty-year investment in the politics of England. He began it as a late-night, party-loving, upper-class unbeliever. He was single and would stay that way happily until he was thirty-seven years old. Then he met Barbara on April 15, 1797. He fell immediately in love. Within eight days he proposed to her, and on May 30 they were married, about six weeks after they met— and stayed married until William died thirty-six years later. In the first eight years of their marriage they had four sons and two daughters. We will come back to William as a family man, because it sheds light on his character and how he endured the political battles of the day.

"The Great Change": The Story of His Conversion

I have skipped over the most important thing, his conversion to a deep, Christian, evangelical faith. It is a great story of the providence of God pursuing a person through seemingly casual choices. On the long holidays when Parliament was not in session, Wilberforce would sometimes travel with friends or family. In the winter of 1784, when he was twenty-five, on an impulse he invited Isaac Milner, his former schoolmaster and friend from grammar school, who was now a tutor in Queens College, Cambridge, to go with him and his mother and sister to the French Riviera. To his amazement Milner turned out to be a convinced Christian without any of the stereotypes that Wilberforce had built up against evangelicals. They talked for hours about the Christian faith.

In another seemingly accidental turn, Wilberforce saw lying in the house where they were staying a copy of Philip Doddridge's *The Rise and Progress of Religion in the Soul* (1745). He asked

Milner about it, and Milner said that it was "one of the best books ever written" and suggested they take it along and read it on the way home.[18] Wilberforce later ascribes a huge influence in his conversion to this book. When he arrived home in February 1785 he "had reached intellectual assent to the Biblical view of man, God and Christ." But he would not yet have claimed what he later described as true Christianity. It was all intellectual. He pushed it to the back of his mind and went on with political and social life.

That summer Wilberforce traveled again with Milner, and they discussed the Greek New Testament for hours. Slowly his "intellectual assent became profound conviction."[19] One of the first manifestations of what he called "the great change"—the conversion—was the contempt he felt for his wealth and the luxury he lived in, especially on these trips between Parliamentary sessions. Seeds were sown almost immediately at the beginning of his Christian life, it seems, of the later passion to help the poor and to turn all his inherited wealth and his naturally high station into a means of blessing the oppressed.

"Highly Dangerous Possessions"

Simplicity and generosity were the mark of his life. Much later, after he was married, he wrote, "By careful management, I should be able to give at least one-quarter of my income to the poor."[20] His sons reported that before he married he was giving away well over a fourth of his income, one year actually giving away £3000 more than he made. He wrote that riches were, "consid-

---

[18] Ibid., p. 34.
[19] Ibid., p. 37.
[20] Betty Steele Everett, *Freedom Fighter: The Story of William Wilberforce* (Fort Washington, PA: Christian Literature Crusade, 1994), p. 68.

ering them as in themselves, acceptable, but, from the infirmity of [our] nature, as highly dangerous possessions; and [we are to value] them chiefly not as instruments of luxury or splendor, but as affording the means of honoring [our] heavenly Benefactor, and lessening the miseries of mankind."[21] This was the way his mind worked: Everything in politics was for the alleviation of misery and the spread of happiness.

The Regret That Leads to Life

By October he was bemoaning the "shapeless idleness" of his past. He was thinking particularly of his time at Cambridge—"the most valuable years of life wasted, and opportunities lost, which can never be recovered."[22] He had squandered his early years in Parliament as well: "The first years I was in Parliament I did nothing—nothing that is to any purpose. My own distinction was my darling object."[23] He was so ashamed of his prior life that he wrote with apparent overstatement, "I was filled with sorrow. I am sure that no human creature could suffer more than I did for some months. It seems indeed it quite affected my reason."[24] He was tormented about what his new Christianity meant for his public life. William Pitt tried to talk him out of becoming an evangelical and argued that this change would "render your talents useless both to yourself and mankind."[25]

---

[21] Wilberforce, *A Practical View of Christianity*, p. 113.
[22] Robert Isaac Wilberforce and Samuel Wilberforce, *The Life of William Wilberforce*, Vol. 1 (London: John Murray, 1838), p. 107.
[23] Pollock, "A Man Who Changed His Times," p. 80.
[24] Pollock, *Wilberforce*, p. 37.
[25] Ibid., p. 38.

Ten Thousand Doubts and Good Counsel

To resolve the anguish he felt over what to do with his life as a Christian, he resolved to risk seeing John Newton on December 7, 1785—a risk because Newton was an evangelical and not admired or esteemed by Wilberforce's colleagues in Parliament. He wrote to Newton on December 2:

> I wish to have some serious conversation with you. . . . I have had ten thousand doubts within myself, whether or not I should discover myself to you; but every argument against it has its foundation in pride. I am sure you will hold yourself bound to let no one living know of this application, or of my visit, till I release you from the obligation. . . . PS Remember that I must be secret, and that the gallery of the House is now so universally attended, that the face of a member of parliament is pretty well known.[26]

It was a historically significant visit. Not only did Newton give encouragement to Wilberforce's faith, but he also urged him not to cut himself off from public life. Wilberforce wrote about the visit:

> After walking about the Square once or twice before I could persuade myself, I called upon old Newton—was much affected in conversing with him—something very pleasing and unaffected in him. He told me he always had hopes and confidence that God would sometime bring me to Him. . . . When I came away I found my mind in a calm, tranquil state, more humbled, and looking more devoutly up to God.[27]

---

[26] Robert Isaac Wilberforce and Samuel Wilberforce, *The Life of William Wilberforce*, abridged edition (London, 1843), p. 47.

[27] Ibid., p. 48.

Wilberforce was relieved that the sixty-year-old Newton urged him not to cut himself off from public life. Newton wrote to Wilberforce two years later: "It is hoped and believed that the Lord has raised you up for the good of His church and for the good of the nation."[28] One marvels at the magnitude of some small occasions when one thinks what hung in the balance in that moment of counsel, in view of what Wilberforce would accomplish for the cause of abolition.

The battle and uncertainties lasted on into the new year, but finally a more settled serenity came over him, and on Easter Day, 1786, the politician for Yorkshire took to the fields to pray and give thanks, as he said in a letter to his sister Sally, "amidst the general chorus with which all nature seems on such a morning to be swelling the song of praise and thanksgiving."[29] It was, he said almost ten years later, as if "to have awakened . . . from a dream, to have recovered, as it were, the use of my reason after a delirium."[30]

With this change came a whole new regimen for the use of his months of recess from Parliament. Beginning not long after his conversion and lasting until he was married eleven years later, he would now spend his days studying "about nine or ten hours a day," typically "breakfasting alone, taking walks alone, dining with the host family and other guests but not joining them in the evening until he 'came down about three-quarters of an hour before bedtime for what supper I wanted.'"[31] "The Bible became his best-loved book and he learned stretches by heart."[32] He was setting out to recover a lot of ground lost to laziness in college.

---

[28] Ibid.
[29] Ibid., p. 39.
[30] Robert Isaac Wilberforce and Samuel Wilberforce, *The Life of William Wilberforce*, Vol. 1, pp. 107-108.
[31] Ibid., p. 43.
[32] Ibid., p. 44.

"God Has Set Before Me Two Great Objects"

Now we turn to what makes Wilberforce so relevant to the cause of racial justice in our day—namely, his lifelong devotion to the cause of abolishing the African slave trade, and then slavery itself. In 1787 Wilberforce wrote a letter in which he estimated that the annual export of slaves from the western coast of Africa for all nations exceeded £100,000.[33] Seventeen years later in 1804 he estimated that for the Guiana importation alone, 12,000-15,000 human beings were enslaved every year the trade continued. One year after his conversion, God's apparent calling on his life had become clear to him. On October 28, 1787, he wrote in his diary, "God Almighty has set before me two great objects, the suppression of the Slave Trade and the Reformation of Manners [morals]."[34]

Soon after Christmas, 1787, a few days before the parliamentary recess, Wilberforce gave notice in the House of Commons that early in the new session he would bring a motion for the abolition of the slave trade. It would be twenty years before he could carry the House of Commons and the House of Lords in putting abolition into law. But the more he studied the matter and the more he heard of the atrocities, the more resolved he became. In May 1789 he spoke to the House about how he came to his conviction: "I confess to you, so enormous, so dreadful, so irremediable did its wickedness appear that my own mind was completely made up for Abolition. . . . Let the consequences be what they would, I from this time determined that I would never rest until I had effected its abolition."[35]

---

[33] Ibid., p. 72
[34] Ibid., p. 69.
[35] Ibid., p. 56.

He embraced the guilt for himself when he said in that same year, "I mean not to accuse anyone but to take the shame upon myself, in common indeed with the whole Parliament of Great Britain, for having suffered this horrid trade to be carried on under their authority. We are all guilty—we ought all to plead guilty, and not to exculpate ourselves by throwing the blame on others."[36]

In 1793 he wrote to a supporter who thought he was growing soft and cautious in the cause, "If I thought the immediate Abolition of the Slave Trade would cause an insurrection in our islands, I should not for an instant remit my most strenuous endeavors. Be persuaded then, I shall still less ever make this grand cause the sport of the caprice, or sacrifice it to motives of political convenience or personal feeling."[37] Three years later, almost ten years after the battle was begun, he wrote:

> The grand object of my parliamentary existence [is the abolition of the slave trade]. . . . Before this great cause all others dwindle in my eyes, and I must say that the *certainty* that I am right *here*, adds greatly to the complacency with which I exert myself in asserting it. If it please God to honor me so far, may I be the instrument of stopping such a course of wickedness and cruelty as never before disgraced a Christian country.[38]

Triumph Over All Opposition

Of course the opposition that raged for these twenty years was because of the financial benefits of slavery to the traders and to

---

[36] Ibid., p. 89.
[37] Ibid., p. 123.
[38] Ibid., p. 143.

the British economy, because of what the plantations in the West Indies produced. They could not conceive of any way to produce without slave labor. This meant that Wilberforce's life was threatened more than once. When he criticized the credibility of a slave ship captain, Robert Norris, the man was enraged, and Wilberforce feared for his life. Short of physical harm, there was the painful loss of friends. Some would no longer fight with him, and they were estranged. Then there was the huge political pressure to back down because of the international political ramifications. For example, if Britain really outlawed slavery, the West Indian colonial assemblies threatened to declare independence from Britain and to federate with the United States. These kinds of financial and political arguments held Parliament captive for decades.

But the night—or I should say early morning—of victory came in 1807. The moral vision and the political momentum for abolition had finally become irresistible. At one point "the House rose almost to a man and turned towards Wilberforce in a burst of Parliamentary cheers. Suddenly, above the roar of 'Hear, hear,' and quite out of order, three hurrahs echoed and echoed while he sat, head bowed, tears streaming down his face."[39] At 4:00 A.M., February 24, 1807, the House divided—Ayes, 283, Noes, 16, Majority for the Abolition 267. And on March 25, 1807, the royal assent was declared. One of Wilberforce's friends wrote, "[Wilberforce] attributes it to the immediate interposition of Providence."[40] In that early morning hour Wilberforce turned to his best friend and colleague, Henry Thornton, and said, "Well, Henry, what shall we abolish next?"[41]

---

[39] Ibid., p. 211.
[40] Ibid., p. 212.
[41] Ibid.

The Battle Was Not Over

Of course the battle wasn't over. And Wilberforce fought on[42] until his death twenty-six years later in 1833. Not only was the *implementation* of the abolition law controversial and difficult, but all it did was abolish the slave *trade*, not slavery itself. That became the next major cause. In 1821 Wilberforce recruited Thomas Fowell Buxton to carry on the fight, and from the sidelines, aged and fragile, he cheered him on. Three months before his death in 1833 he was persuaded to propose a last petition against slavery. "I had never thought to appear in public again, but it shall never be said that William Wilberforce is silent while the slaves require his help."[43]

The decisive vote of victory for that one came on July 26, 1833, only three days before Wilberforce died. Slavery itself was outlawed in the British colonies. Minor work on the legislation took several more days. "It is a singular fact," Buxton said, "that on the very night on which we were successfully engaged in the House of Commons, in passing the clause of the Act of Emancipation—one of the most important clauses ever enacted . . . the spirit of our friend left the world. The day which was the termination of his labors was the termination of his life."[44]

William Cowper wrote a sonnet[45] to celebrate Wilberforce's labor for the slaves which begins with the lines,

---

[42] In 1823 Wilberforce wrote a fifty-six-page booklet, "Appeal to the Religion, Justice and Humanity of the Inhabitants of the British Empire in Behalf of the Negro Slaves in the West Indies." Ibid., p. 285.

[43] Pollock, "A Man Who Changed His Times," p. 90.

[44] Ibid., p. 91.

[45]
> Thy country, Wilberforce, with just disdain
> Hears thee by cruel men and impious call'd
> Fanatic, for thy zeal to loose the enthrall'd
> From exile, public sale, and slavery's chain.
> Friend of the poor, the wrong'd, the fetter-gall'd,
> Fear not lest labor such as thine be vain.
> Thou hast achieved a part: hast gained the ear
> Of Britain's senate to thy glorious cause;

Thy country, Wilberforce, with just disdain,
Hears thee by cruel men and impious call'd
Fanatic, for thy zeal to loose the enthrall'd
From exile, public sale, and slavery's chain.
Friend of the poor, the wrong'd, the fetter-gall'd,
Fear not lest labor such as thine be vain.

Wilberforce's friend and sometimes pastor, William Jay, wrote a tribute with this accurate prophecy, "His disinterested, self-denying, laborious, undeclining efforts in this cause of justice and humanity . . . will call down the blessings of millions; and ages yet to come will glory in his memory."[46]

But He Was Not a Single-Issue Candidate

I must not give the impression that all Wilberforce cared about or worked for was the abolition of slavery. In fact, the diversity of the evangelistic and benevolent causes he labored to advance makes his devotion to abolition all the more wonderful. Most of us make the multiplicity of demands an excuse for not giving ourselves to any one great cause over the long haul. Not so with Wilberforce.[47] There was a steady stream of action to alleviate pain and bring the greater social (and eternal!) good. "At one stage he was active in sixty-nine different initiatives."[48]

His involvements ranged widely. He was involved with the

Hope smiles, joy springs; and though cold Caution pause,
And weave delay, the better hour is near
That shall remunerate thy toils severe,
By peace for Afric, fenced with British laws.
Enjoy what thou has won, esteem and love
From all the Just on earth, and all the Blest above.

[46] William Jay, *The Autobiography of William Jay*, eds. George Redford and John Angell James (Edinburgh: The Banner of Truth Trust, 1974, orig. 1854), p. 315.
[47] See pp. 118-119.
[48] Pollock, "A Man Who Changed His Times," p. 89.

British Foreign Bible Society, the Church Missionary Society, the Society for the Manufacturing Poor, and the Society for the Better Observance of Sunday. He worked for the alleviation of harsh child labor conditions (like the use of small boys by chimney sweeps to climb up chimneys), for agricultural reform that supplied affordable food to the poor, for prison reform and the restriction of capital punishment from cavalier use, and for the prevention of cruelty to animals.[49] On and on the list could go. In fact, it was the very diversity of the needs and crimes and injustices that confirmed his evangelical conviction that one must finally deal with the *root* of all these ills if one is to have a lasting and broad influence for good. That is why, as we have seen, he wrote his book, *A Practical View of Christianity.*

The Personal Evangelism of a Politician

Alongside all his social engagements, he carried on a steady relational ministry, as we might call it, seeking to win his unbelieving colleagues to personal faith in Jesus Christ. Even though he said, "the grand business of [clergymen's] lives should be winning souls from the power of Satan unto God, and compared with it all other pursuits are mean and contemptible,"[50] he did not believe that this was the responsibility *only* of the clergy. In a chance meet-

---

[49] Of course, concern for animals is not the apex of the moral life. But it may be indicative of a character that supports far more significant mercies. As the Scripture says, "Whoever is righteous has regard for the life of his beast, but the mercy of the wicked is cruel" (Proverbs 12:10). So the following personal recollection of Wilberforce's grandson is not insignificant. "Wilberforce was also a great lover of animals and a founder of the Royal Society for the Prevention of Cruelty to Animals, which led me to a lovely story. His last surviving grandson told me how his father as a small boy was walking with Wilberforce on a hill near Bath when they saw a poor carthorse being cruelly whipped by the carter as he struggled to pull a load of stone up the hill. The little liberator expostulated with the carter who began to swear at him and tell him to mind his own business, and so forth. Suddenly the carter stopped and said, 'Are you Mr. Wilberforce? . . . Then I will never beat my horse again!'" Pollock, "A Man Who Changed His Times," p. 90.

[50] Pollock, *Wilberforce*, p. 148.

ing with James Boswell, Samuel Johnson's biographer, he spent time into the night dealing with him about his soul, but seemed not to be able to get beyond some serious feelings.[51] He grieved for his longtime unbelieving parliamentary friend Charles Fox and longed "that I might be the instrument of bringing him to the knowledge of Christ!"[52]

He anonymously visited in prison a famous infidel named Richard Carlile who was imprisoned for his blasphemous writings. When Wilberforce took out a small Bible, Carlile said, "I wish to have nothing to do with that book; and you cannot wonder at this, for if that book be true, I am damned forever!" To which Wilberforce replied, "No, no, Mr. Carlile, according to that book, there is hope for all who will seek for mercy and forgiveness; for it assures us that God hath no pleasure in the death of him that dieth."[53]

Missions and Mercy Across the Miles

His zeal for the Gospel and his compassion for perishing people were extended from personal relationships at home to places as far away as India. On April 14, 1806 he wrote, "Next to the Slave Trade, I have long thought our making no effort to introduce the blessings of religious and moral improvement among our subjects in the East, the greatest of our *national* crimes."[54] Seven years later "Wilberforce ... enthralled the House ... with the cause of Christian missions in India."[55] The Englishman William Carey had to live in Serampore,

---

[51] Ibid., p. 119.
[52] Ibid., p. 205.
[53] Ibid., p. 258.
[54] Ibid., p. 235.
[55] Ibid., pp. 235-236.

a Danish enclave in India, until Wilberforce triumphed in 1813 when the prohibition of evangelism in British colonies in India was lifted by the East India Company Charter, which now guaranteed liberty to propagate the Christian Faith. "Parliament had opened a fast-locked door and it was Wilberforce who had turned the key, in a speech which Lord Erskine said 'deserves a place in the library of every man of letters, even if he were an atheist.'"[56] Even at this huge distance Wilberforce brought together evangelistic zeal and concern for social justice. He bemoaned the practice of *suttee* and would read out at his supper table the names of women who had been killed on the funeral fires of their husband; he knew something of the tyrannies of the caste system.[57]

The link that Wilberforce saw between social good and eternal good is seen in the case of the remote English people of Mendip Hills. In 1789, when Wilberforce saw the terrible plight of these backward, poor, unpastored people, he urged the philanthropist Hannah More to conceive a plan that he would pay for. She worked out a plan to establish a school and teach them to read. She wrote to Wilberforce, "What a comfort I feel in looking around on these starving and half-naked multitudes, to think that by your liberality many of them may be fed and clothed; and O if but one soul is rescued from eternal misery how we may rejoice over it in another state!"[58]

The breadth of his heart and the diversity of his action beckons us all the more to ponder the source of his constancy, especially in a cause that was at first unpopular and easily defeated—the economically advantageous slave trade.

---

[56] Ibid., p. 238.
[57] Ibid., p. 236.
[58] Ibid., pp. 92-93.

Extraordinary Endurance

Consider now the remarkable perseverance of this man in the cause of justice. I admit, this is what drew me to Wilberforce in the first place—his reputation as a man who simply would not give up when the cause was just.

There was a ray of hope in 1804 that things might be moving to a success (three years before it actually came), but Wilberforce wrote, "I have been so often disappointed, that I rejoice with trembling and shall scarcely dare to be confident till I actually see the Order in the Gazette."[59] But these repeated defeats of his plans did not defeat *him*. His adversaries complained that "Wilberforce jumped up whenever they knocked him down."[60] One of them in particular put it like this: "It is necessary to watch him as he is blessed with a very sufficient quantity of that Enthusiastic spirit, which is so far from yielding that it grows more vigorous from blows."[61]

When John Wesley was eighty-seven years old (in 1790) he wrote to Wilberforce and said, "Unless God has raised you up for this very thing, you will be worn out by the opposition of man and devils. But if God be for you, who can be against you."[62] Two years later Wilberforce wrote in a letter, "I daily become more sensible that my work must be affected by constant and regular exertions rather than by sudden and violent ones."[63] In other words, with fifteen years to go in the first phase of the battle, he

---

[59] Ibid., p. 189.
[60] Ibid., p. 123.
[61] Ibid., p. 105.
[62] Ibid.
[63] Ibid., p. 116.

knew that only a marathon mentality, rather than a sprint mentality, would prevail in this cause.

Six years later in 1800, on his forty-first birthday, as he reded-
icated himself to his calling, he prayed, "Oh Lord, purify my
soul from all its stains. Warm my heart with the love of thee, animate my sluggish nature and fix my inconstancy, and volatility,
that I may not be weary in well doing."[64] God answered that
prayer, and the entire western world may be glad that Wilberforce
was granted constancy and perseverance in his labors, especially
his endurance in the cause of justice against the sin of slavery
and racism.

Obstacles

What makes Wilberforce's perseverance through four decades of
political action in the single-minded cause of justice so remarkable is not only the length of it but the obstacles he had to sur-
mount in the battle for abolition of the slave trade and then of
slavery itself. I have mentioned the massive financial interests on
the other side, both personal and national. It seemed utterly
unthinkable to Parliament that Britain could prosper without what
the plantations of the West Indies provided. Then there were the
international politics and how Britain was positioned in relation
to France, Portugal, Brazil, and the new nation, the United States
of America. If one nation, like Britain, unilaterally abolished the
slave trade, but the others did not, it would simply mean—so the
argument ran—that power and wealth would be transmitted to the
other nations and Britain would be weakened internationally.

---

[64] Ibid., p. 179.

Slander

In February 1807, when Wilberforce, at forty-seven, led the first victory over the slave trade, it was true that as John Pollock says, "His achievement brought him a personal moral authority with public and Parliament above any living man."[65] But, as every public person knows, and as Jesus promised,[66] the best of men will be maligned for the best of actions.

On one occasion in 1820, thirteen years after the first victory, he took a very controversial position with regard to Queen Caroline's marital unfaithfulness and experienced a dramatic public outrage against him. He wrote in his diary on July 20, 1820, "What a lesson it is to a man not to set his heart on low popularity when after 40 years [of] disinterested public service, I am believed by the Bulk to be a Hypocritical Rascal. O what a comfort it is to have to fly for refuge to a God of unchangeable truth and love."[67]

Probably the severest criticism he ever received was from a slavery-defending adversary named William Cobett, in August 1823, who turned Wilberforce's commitment to abolition into a moral liability by claiming that Wilberforce pretended to care for slaves from Africa but cared nothing about the "wage slaves"—the wretched poor of England.

> You seem to have a great affection for the fat and lazy and laughing and singing and dancing Negroes. . . . [But] Never have you done one single act in favor of the labor-

---

[65] Ibid., p. 215. Wilberforce's own assessment of the resulting moral authority was this (written in a letter March 3, 1807): "The authority which the great principles of justice and humanity have received will be productive of benefit in all shapes and directions."

[66] Matthew 10:25, "If they have called the master of the house Beelzebul, how much more will they malign those of his household."

[67] Pollock, *Wilberforce*, p. 276.

ers of this country [a statement Cobett knew to be false]. . . . You make your appeal in Picadilly, London, amongst those who are wallowing in luxuries, proceeding from the labor of the people. You should have gone to the gravel-pits, and made your appeal to the wretched creatures with bits of sacks around their shoulders, and with hay-bands round their legs; you should have gone to the roadside, and made your appeal to the emaciated, half-dead things who are there cracking stones to make the roads as level as a die for the tax eaters to ride on. What an insult it is, and what an unfeeling, what a cold-blooded hypocrite must he be that can send it forth; what an insult to call upon people under the name of free British laborers; to appeal to them in behalf of Black slaves, when these free British laborers; these poor, mocked, degraded wretches, would be happy to lick the dishes and bowls, out of which the Black slaves have breakfasted, dined, or supped.[68]

A Father's Pain

But far more painful than any of these criticisms were the heartaches of family life. Every leader knows that almost any external burden is bearable if the family is whole and happy. But when the family is torn, all burdens are doubled. Wilberforce and his wife Barbara were very different. "While he was always cheerful, Barbara was often depressed and pessimistic. She finally worried herself into very bad health which lasted the rest of her life." And other women who knew her said she "whined when William was not right beside her."[69]

When their oldest, William, was at Trinity College, Cambridge,

---

[68] Ibid., p. 287.
[69] Everett, *Freedom Fighter*, pp. 64-65.

he fell away from the Christian faith and gave no evidence of the precious experience his father called "the great change." Wilberforce wrote on January 10, 1819, "O that my poor dear William might be led by thy grace, O God." On March 11 he poured out his grief:

> Oh my poor Willm. How strange he can make so miserable those who love him best and whom really he loves. His soft nature makes him the sport of his companions, and the wicked and idle naturally attach themselves like dust and cleave like burrs. I go to pray for him. Alas, could I love my Savior more and serve him, God would hear my prayer and turn his heart.[70]

He got word from Henry Venn that William was not reading for his classes at Cambridge but was spending his father's allowance foolishly. Wilberforce agonized and decided to cut off his allowance, have him suspended from school, put him with another family, and not allow him to come home. "Alas my poor Willm! How sad to be compelled to banish my eldest son."[71] Even when William finally came back to faith, it grieved Wilberforce that three of his sons became very high-church Anglicans with little respect for the dissenting church that Wilberforce, even as an Anglican, loved so much for its evangelical truth and life.[72]

On top of this family burden came the death of his daughter Barbara. In the autumn of 1821, at thirty-two, she was diag-

---

[70] Pollock, *Wilberforce*, p. 267.

[71] Ibid., p. 268. From the diary, April 11, 1819.

[72] The official biography written by his sons is defective in portraying Wilberforce in a false light as opposed to dissenters, when in fact some of his best friends and spiritual counselors were among their number. After Wilberforce's death, three of his sons became Roman Catholic.

nosed with consumption (tuberculosis). She died five days after Christmas. Wilberforce wrote to a friend, "Oh my dear Friend, it is in such seasons as these that the value of the promises of the Word of God are ascertained both by the dying and the attendant relatives. . . . The assured persuasion of Barbara's happiness has taken away the sting of death."[73] He sounds strong, but the blow shook his remaining strength, and in March 1822, he wrote to his son, "I am confined by a new malady, the Gout."[74]

His Bad Eyes, Ulcerated Bowels, Opium, and Curved Spine

The word "new" in that letter signals that Wilberforce labored under some other extraordinary physical handicaps that made his long perseverance in political life all the more remarkable. He wrote in 1788 that his eyes were so bad "[I can scarcely] see how to direct my pen." The humorous side to this was that "he was often shabbily dressed, according to one friend, and his clothes sometimes were put on crookedly because he never looked into a mirror. Since his eyes were too bad to let him see his image clearly, he didn't bother to look at all!"[75] But in fact, there was little humor in his eye disease. In later years he frequently mentioned the "peculiar complaint of my eyes," that he could not see well enough to read or write during the first hours of the day. "This was a symptom of a slow buildup of morphine poisoning."[76]

This ominous assessment was owing to the fact that from 1788 doctors prescribed daily opium pills to Wilberforce to con-

---

[73] Ibid., p. 280.
[74] Ibid.
[75] Everett, *Freedom Fighter*, p. 69.
[76] Pollock, *Wilberforce*, p. 81.

trol the debility of his ulcerative colitis. The medicine was viewed in his day as a "pure drug," and it never occurred to any of his enemies to reproach him for his dependence on opium to control his illness.[77] "Yet effects there must have been," Pollock observes. "Wilberforce certainly grew more untidy, indolent (as he often bemoaned) and absent-minded as his years went on though not yet in old age; it is proof of the strength of his will that he achieved so much under a burden which neither he nor his doctors understood."[78]

In 1812 Wilberforce decided to resign his seat in Yorkshire— not to leave politics, but to take a less demanding seat from a smaller county. He gave his reason as the desire to spend more time with his family. The timing was good, because in the next two years, on top of his colon problem and eye problem and emerging lung problem, he developed a curvature of the spine. "One shoulder began to slope; and his head fell forward, a little more each year until it rested on his chest unless lifted by conscious movement: he could have looked grotesque were it not for the charm of his face and the smile which hovered about his mouth."[79] For the rest of his life he wore a brace beneath his clothes that most people knew nothing about.[80]

---

[77] Ibid., pp. 79-81 for a full discussion of the place of opium in his life and culture. "Wilberforce resisted the craving and only raised his dosage suddenly when there were severe bowel complaints." In April 1818, thirty years after the first prescription, "Wilberforce noted in his diary that his dose 'is still as it has long been,' a pill three times a day (after breakfast, after tea, and bedtime) each of four grains. Twelve grains daily is a good but not outstanding dose and very far from addiction after such a length of time."

[78] Ibid., p. 81.

[79] Ibid., p. 234.

[80] "He was obliged to wear 'a steel girdle cased in leather and an additional part to support the arms. . . . It must be handled carefully, the steel being so elastic as to be easily broken.' He took a spare one ('wrapped up for decency's sake in a towel') wherever he stayed; the fact that he lived in a steel frame for his last 15 or 18 years might have remained unknown had he not left behind at the Lord Calthorpe's Suffolk home, Ampton Hall, the more comfortable of the two. 'How gracious is God,' Wilberforce remarked in the letter asking for its return, 'in giving us such mitigations and helps for our infirmities.'" Ibid., pp. 233-234.

He Did Not Fight Alone

What were the roots of Wilberforce's perseverance under these kinds of burdens and obstacles? Before we focus on the decisive root, we must pay due respect to the power of camaraderie in the cause of righteousness. Many people associate Wilberforce's name with the term *Clapham Sect*. That term was not used during his lifetime. But the band that it referred to were "tagged 'the Saints' by their contemporaries in Parliament—uttered by some with contempt, while by others with deep admiration."[81] The group centered around the church of John Venn, rector of Clapham, a suburb of London. It included Wilberforce, Henry Thornton, James Stephen, Zachary Macaulay, Granville Sharp, John Shore (Lord Teignmouth), and Charles Grant.

Henry Thornton, banker and economist, was Wilberforce's "dearest friend"[82] and cousin. In the spring of 1792 he "suggested to Wilberforce that they set up a 'chummery' at Battersea Rise, the small estate that Thornton had bought in Clapham. Each would pay his share of the housekeeping, and this became Wilberforce's home for the next five years."[83]

> At certain points these friends . . . resided in adjoining homes in a suburb of London called Clapham Common, functioning as one. In fact, their *esprit de corps* was so evident and contagious that whether geographically together or not, they operated like "a meeting which never adjourned." The achievement of Wilberforce's vision is largely attributable to the value he and his colleagues

---

[81] J. Douglas Holladay, "A Life of Significance," in *Character Counts*, p. 72.
[82] Pollock, *Wilberforce*, p. 102.
[83] Ibid., p. 117.

placed on harnessing their diverse skills while submitting their egos for the greater public good.[84]

Wilberforce did not set out to gather a strategic band of comrades to strengthen his cause. It came together because of the kind of man he was and the compelling vision he had of what a public Christian life should be. He had a deep "love of conversation and could hardly resist prolonging a chat and kept many late hours leaving the mornings to less important things."[85] This love of company and great capacity for friendship combined with the power of his vision for public righteousness to attract "the Saints." Together they accomplished more than any could have done on his own. "William Wilberforce is proof that a man can change his times, though he cannot do it alone."[86]

The Deeper Root of Childlike Joy

But there is a deeper root of Wilberforce's endurance than camaraderie. It is the root of childlike, child-loving, self-forgetting joy in Christ. The testimonies and evidence of this in Wilberforce's life are many. A certain Miss Sullivan wrote to a friend about Wilberforce around 1815: "By the tones of his voice and expression of his countenance he showed that *joy* was the prevailing feature of his own mind, joy springing from entireness of trust in the Savior's merits and from love to God and man.... His joy was quite penetrating."[87]

On the occasion of Wilberforce's death, Joseph Brown spoke

---

[84] Holladay, "A Life of Significance," p. 72.
[85] Pollock, *Wilberforce*, pp. 118-119.
[86] Pollock, "A Man Who Changed His Times," p. 88.
[87] Ibid., p. 152.

in St. Paul's Church in Middlesex. He focused on this attribute of the man.

> He was also a most cheerful Christian. His harp appeared to be always in tune; no "gloomy atmosphere of a melancholy moroseness" surrounded him; his sun appeared to be always shining: hence he was remarkably fond of singing hymns, both in family prayer and when alone. He would say, "A Christian should have joy and peace in believing [Romans 15:13]: It is his duty to abound in praise."[88]

The poet Robert Southey said, "I never saw any other man who seemed to enjoy such a perpetual serenity and sunshine of spirit. In conversing with him, you feel assured that there is no guile in him; that if ever there was a good man and happy man on earth, he was one."[89] In 1881 Dorothy Wordsworth, sister of the famous romantic poet, wrote, "Though shattered in constitution and feeble in body he is as lively and animated as in the days of his youth."[90] His sense of humor and delight in all that was good was vigorous and unmistakable. In 1824 John Russell gave a speech in the Commons with such wit that Wilberforce "collapsed in helpless laughter."[91]

This playful side made him a favorite of children, as they were favorites of his. His best friend's daughter, Marianne Thornton, said that often "Wilberforce would interrupt his serious talks with her father and romp with her in the lawn. 'His love for and enjoyment in all children was remarkable.'"[92] Once,

---

[88] *The Christian Observer*, January 1834, London, p. 63.
[89] Jay, *The Autobiography of William Jay*, p. 317.
[90] Pollock, *Wilberforce*, p. 267.
[91] Ibid., p. 289
[92] Ibid., p. 183.

when his own children were playing upstairs and he was frustrated at having misplaced a letter, he heard a great din of children shouting. His guest thought he would be perturbed. Instead he smiled and said, "What a blessing to have these dear children! Only think what a relief, amidst other hurries, to hear their voices and know they are well."[93]

> He was an unusual father for his day. Most fathers who had the wealth and position he did rarely saw their children. Servants and a governess took care of the children, and they were to be out of sight most of the time. Instead, William insisted on eating as many meals as possible with the children, and he joined in their games. He played marbles and Blindman's Bluff and ran races with them. In the games, the children treated him like one of them.[94]

Southey once visited the house when all the children were there and wrote that he marveled at "the pell-mell, topsy-turvy and chaotic confusion" of the Wilberforce apartments in which the wife sat like Patience on a monument while her husband "frisks about as if every vein in his body were filled with quicksilver."[95] Another visitor in 1816, Joseph John Gurney, a Quaker, stayed a week with Wilberforce and recalled later, "As he walked about the house he was generally humming the tune of a hymn or Psalm as if he could not contain his pleasurable feelings of thankfulness and devotion."[96]

---

[93] Ibid., p. 232.
[94] Everett, *Freedom Fighter*, p. 70.
[95] Pollock, *Wilberforce*, p. 267.
[96] Ibid., p. 261.

Interested in All and Interesting to All

There was in this childlike love of children and joyful freedom from care a deeply healthy self-forgetfulness. Richard Wellesley, Duke of Wellington, wrote after a meeting with Wilberforce, "You have made me so entirely forget you are a great man by seeming to forget it yourself in all our intercourse."[97] The effect of this self-forgetting joy was another mark of mental and spiritual health, namely, a joyful ability to see all the good in the world instead of being consumed by one's own problems (even when those problems were huge).

Wilberforce's friend, James Mackintosh, spoke of that remarkable trait of healthy, adult childlikeness, namely, the freedom from self-absorption that is interested in the simplest and most ordinary things:

> If I were called upon to describe Wilberforce in one word, I should say that he was the most "amusable" man I ever met in my life. Instead of having to think of what subjects will interest him it is perfectly impossible to hit one that does not. I never saw anyone who touched life at so many points and this is the more remarkable in a man who is supposed to live absorbed in the contemplation of a future state. When he was in the House of Commons he seemed to have the freshest mind of any man there. There was all the charm of youth about him.[98]

His Presence Fatal to Dullness

This must have been the way many viewed him, for another of his contemporaries, James Stephen, recalled after Wilberforce's

---

[97] Ibid., p. 236.
[98] Holladay, "A Life of Significance," p. 74.

death, "Being himself amused and interested by everything, whatever he said became amusing or interesting. . . . His presence was as fatal to dullness as to immorality. His mirth was as irresistible as the first laughter of childhood."[99]

Here is a great key to his perseverance and effectiveness. His presence was "fatal to dullness . . . [and] immorality." In other words, his indomitable joy moved others to be happy and good. He remarked in his book *A Practical View of Christianity*, "The path of virtue is that also of real interest and of solid enjoyment."[100] In other words, "It is more blessed to give than to receive" (Acts 20:35). He sustained himself and swayed others by his joy. If a man can rob you of your joy, he can rob you of your usefulness. Wilberforce's joy was indomitable and therefore he was a compelling Christian and politician all his life. This was the strong root of his endurance.

Hannah More, his wealthy friend and a patron of many of his schemes for doing good, said to him, "I declare I think you are serving God by being yourself agreeable . . . to worldly but well-disposed people, who would never be attracted to religion by grave and severe divines, even if such fell in their way."[101] In fact, I think one of the reasons Wilberforce did not like to use the word "Calvinist,"[102] although the faith and doctrines he expresses seem

---

[99] Pollock, *Wilberforce*, p. 185.

[100] Wilberforce, *A Practical View of Christianity*, p. 12.

[101] Ibid., p. 119.

[102] He disliked anything that "produced hard and sour divinity." He wrote in a letter on May 26, 1814, "There are no names or party distinctions in heaven." Though he wrote in 1821, "I myself am no Calvinist," he "urged the claims of Calvinist clergy for bishoprics." In 1799 he had written, "God knows, I say it solemnly, that it has been (particularly of late) and shall be more and more my endeavor to promote the cordial and vigorous and systematical exertions of all friends of the essentials of Christianity, softening prejudices, healing divisions and striving to substitute a rational and an honest zeal for fundamentals, in place of a hot party spirit." Pollock, *Wilberforce*, p. 153. More than once he was heard to say, "Though I am an Episcopalian by education and conviction, I yet feel such a oneness and sympathy with the cause of God at large, that nothing would be more delightful than my communing, once every year, with every church that holds the Head, even Christ." Jay, *The Autobiography of William Jay*, pp. 298-299.

to line up with the Calvinism of Whitefield and Newton,[103] was this very thing: Calvinists had the reputation of being joyless.

A certain Lord Carrington apparently expressed to Wilberforce his mistrust of joy. Wilberforce responded:

> My grand objection to the religious system still held by many who declare themselves orthodox Churchmen. . . is, that it tends to render Christianity so much a system of prohibitions rather than of privilege and hopes, and thus the injunction to rejoice, so strongly enforced in the New Testament, is practically neglected, and Religion is made to wear a forbidding and gloomy air and not one of peace and hope and joy.[104]

Joy Is Our "Bounden Duty"

Here is a clear statement of Wilberforce's conviction that joy is not optional. It is an "injunction . . . strongly enforced in the New Testament." Or as he says elsewhere, "We can scarcely indeed look into any part of the sacred volume without meeting abundant proofs, that it is the religion of the Affections which God particularly requires. . . . Joy . . . is enjoined on us as our bounden duty and commended to us as our acceptable worship. . . . A cold . . . unfeeling heart is represented as highly criminal."[105]

---

[103] Many of his closest and most admired friends were Calvinists—for example, Hannah More and William Jay. He used his influence to promote Calvinists to bishoprics. When he sought out a church to attend, he often chose to sit under the ministry of Calvinists—for example, Thomas Scott, "one of the most determined Calvinists in England" (Pollock, *Wilberforce*, p. 153), and William Jay. He believed in the absolute sovereignty of God over all the pleasures and pain of the world ("It has pleased God to visit my dearest wife with a very dangerous fever." Ibid., p. 179). He knew that his own repentance was a gift of God ("May I, Oh God, be enabled to repent and turn to thee with my whole heart. I am now flying from thee." Ibid., p. 150). He loved the essay on regeneration by the Calvinist John Witherspoon and wrote a preface for it (Jay, *The Autobiography of William Jay*, p. 298). As I completed his book, *A Practical View of Christianity*, I could not recall a single sentence that a Calvinist like John Newton or George Whitefield or Charles Spurgeon could not agree with.

[104] Pollock, *Wilberforce*, p. 46.

[105] Wilberforce, *A Practical View of Christianity*, pp. 45-46. I cannot let these sentences pass without pointing out the poetic power of Wilberforce's diction. Did you notice how he put

So for Wilberforce, joy was both a means of survival and perseverance on the one hand, and a deep act of submission, obedience, and worship on the other hand. Joy in Christ was commanded. And joy in Christ was the only way to flourish fruitfully through decades of temporary defeat. It was a deep root of endurance. "Never were there times," he wrote, "which inculcated more forcibly than those in which we live, the wisdom of seeking happiness beyond the reach of human vicissitudes."[106]

But What About the Hard Times?

The word "seeking" is important. It is not as though Wilberforce succeeded perfectly in "attaining" the fullest measure of joy. There were great battles in the soul as well as in Parliament. For example, in March 1788, after a serious struggle with colitis he seemed to enter into a "dark night of the soul." "Corrupt imaginations are perpetually rising in my mind and innumerable fears close me in on every side."[107] We get a glimpse of how he fought for joy in these times from what he wrote in his notebook of prayers:

> Lord, thou knowest that no strength, wisdom or contrivance of human power can signify, or relieve me. It is in thy power alone to deliver me. I fly to thee for succor and support, O Lord let it come speedily; give me full proof of thy Almighty power; I am in great troubles, insurmountable by me; but to thee slight and inconsiderable; look upon me O Lord with compassion and mercy, and

---

parallel consonant sounds together? "Joy . . . enjoined. Commended . . . as acceptable. Cold . . . criminal." This kind of thing runs through all his writing and signals a passion to make his words pleasing and effective even as they instruct.

[106] Ibid., p. 239.
[107] Pollock, *Wilberforce*, p. 82.

restore me to rest, quietness, and comfort, in the world, or in another by removing me hence into a state of peace and happiness. Amen.[108]

Less devastating than "the dark night" were the recurrent disappointments with his own failures. But even as we read his self-indictments, we hear the hope of victory that sustained him and restored him to joy again and again. For example, in January 13, 1798, he wrote in his diary:

> Three or four times have I most grievously broke my resolutions since I last took up my pen. Alas! alas! how miserable a wretch am I! How infatuated, how dead to every better feeling yet—yet—yet—may I, Oh God, be enabled to repent and turn to thee with my whole heart, I am now flying from thee. Thou hast been above all measure gracious and forgiving.[109]

Unwearied Endeavor to Relish God

When Wilberforce pressed his readers to "unwearied endeavor" for more "relish" of heavenly things—that is, when he urged them to fight for joy—he was doing what he had learned from long experience. He wrote:

> [The true Christian] walks in the ways of Religion, not by constraint, but willingly; they are to him not only safe, but comfortable, "ways of pleasantness as well as of peace" [Proverbs 3:17]. . . . With earnest prayers, there-

---

[108] Ibid., pp. 81-82.

[109] Ibid., p. 150. He confesses again after a sarcastic rejoinder in the Commons, "In what a fermentation of spirits was I on the night of answering Courtenay. How jealous of character and greedy of applause. Alas, alas! Create in me a clean heart, O God, and renew a right spirit within me" (p. 167).

fore, for the Divine Help, with jealous circumspection and resolute self-denial, he guards against, and abstains from, whatever might be likely again to darken his enlightened judgment, or to vitiate his reformed taste; thus making it his unwearied endeavor to grow in the knowledge and love of heavenly things, and to obtain a warmer admiration, and a more cordial relish of their excellence. . . .[110]

There was in Wilberforce, as in all the most passionate saints, a holy dread of losing his "reformed taste"[111] for spiritual reality. This dread gave rise to "earnest prayers . . . resolute self-denial" and rigorous abstinence from anything that would rob him of the greater joys. He illustrated this dread with the earthly pleasure of "honor." "[The] Christian . . . dreads, lest his supreme affections being thereby gratified [with human praise], it should be hereafter said to him 'remember that thou in thy life-time receivedst thy good things'" (Luke 16:25).[112]

He speaks of "self-denial" exactly the way Jesus did, not as an end in itself, but as a means to the highest pleasures. The mass of nominal Christians of his day did not understand this. And it was the root of their worldliness. "Pleasure and Religion are contradictory terms with the bulk of nominal Christians."[113] But for Wilberforce it was the opposite. The heart and power of true religion—and the root of righteous political endurance—was spiritual pleasure. "O! little do they know of the true measure of enjoyment, who can compare these delightful complacencies with the frivolous pleasures of dissipation, or the coarse gratifications

---

[110] Ibid., pp. 102-103.
[111] The word "reformed" does not refer here to "Calvinistic," but simply to a spiritual taste that was once worldly and now has been "re-formed" into a spiritual taste for spiritual things.
[112] Ibid., p. 122.
[113] Ibid., p. 103.

of sensuality.... The nominal Christian ... knows not the sweetness of the delights with which true Christianity repays those trifling sacrifices."[114] That is what he calls true self-denial—"trifling sacrifices"—just as the apostle Paul called all his earthly treasures "rubbish, in order that I may gain Christ" (Philippians 3:8).

Joy in Christ was so crucial to living the Christian life and persevering in political justice that Wilberforce fought for it with relentless vigilance. "[The Christian's] watch must thus during life know no termination, because the enemy will ever be at hand; so it must be the more close and vigilant, because he is nowhere free from danger, but is on every side open to attack."[115] Therefore, when we say that Wilberforce's happiness was unshakable and undefeatable because it was beyond the reach of human vicissitudes, we don't mean it was beyond struggle; we mean he had learned the secret of "the good fight" (1 Timothy 6:12), and that his embattled joy reasserted itself in and after every tumult in society and in the soul.

Rooting Joy in Truth in the "Retired Hours"

The durable delights in God and the desires for the fullness of Christ that sustained Wilberforce's life did not just happen. He speaks of "the cultivation of . . . desire."[116] There were roots in doctrine. And the link between life and doctrine was prayer. He spoke in his book on Christianity of descending to the world from the "retired hours":

> Thus, at chosen seasons, the Christian exercises himself, and when, from this elevated region he descends into the plain below, and mixes in the bustle of life, he still retains

---

[114] Ibid., p. 237.
[115] Ibid., p. 123.
[116] Wilberforce, *A Practical View of Christianity*, p. 122.

the impressions of his retired hours. By these he realizes to himself the unseen world: he accustoms himself to speak and act as in the presence of "an innumerable company of angels, and of the spirits of just men made perfect, and of God the Judge of all" [Hebrews 12:22-23].[117]

He was writing here out of his own experience. He could not conceal from others his commitment to personal prayer and private devotion. This was one of the main focuses in the funeral sermon by Joseph Brown:

Persons of the highest distinction were frequently at his breakfast-table, but he never made his appearance till he had concluded his own meditations, reading his Bible, and prayer; always securing, as it were, to God, or rather to his own soul, I believe, the first hour of the morning. Whoever surrounded his breakfast-table, however distinguished the individuals, they were invited to join the family circle in family prayer. In reference to his own soul, I am informed, he set apart days, or a part of them, on which he had received particular mercies, for especial prayer. Not only did he pray in his closet, and with his family but if his domestics were ill, at their bed-side— there was their valued master praying with them—praying for them.[118]

He counseled his readers to "rise on the wings of contemplation, until the praises and censures of men die away upon the ear, and the still small voice of conscience is no longer drowned by the din of this nether world."[119] So the question is: contempla-

---

[117] Ibid., p. 123.
[118] *The Christian Observer*, January 1834, London, p. 63.
[119] Wilberforce, *A Practical View of Christianity*, p. 122.

tion on what? Where did Wilberforce go to replenish his soul? If his childlike, child-loving, self-forgetting, indomitable joy was a life-giving root for his endurance in the lifelong fight for abolition, what, we might say, is the root of the root? Or what was the solid ground where the root was planted?

The Gigantic Truths of the Gospel

The main burden of Wilberforce's book, *A Practical View of Christianity*, is to show that true Christianity, which consists in these new, indomitable spiritual affections for Christ, is rooted in the great doctrines of the Bible about sin and Christ and faith.[120] "Let him then who would abound and grow in this Christian principle, be much conversant with the great doctrines of the Gospel."[121] "From the neglect of these peculiar doctrines arise the main practical errors of the bulk of professed Christians. These gigantic truths retained in view, would put to shame the littleness of their dwarfish morality. . . . The whole superstructure of Christian morals is grounded on their deep and ample basis."[122] There is a "perfect harmony between the leading doctrines and the practical precepts of Christianity."[123] And thus it is a "fatal habit"—so common in his day and ours—"to consider Christian morals as distinct from Christian doctrines."[124]

---

[120] See p. 118.
[121] Ibid., p. 170.
[122] Ibid., pp. 166-167.
[123] Ibid., p. 182.
[124] Ibid., p. 198.

Christ Our Righteousness

More specifically, it is the achievement of God through the death of Christ that is at the center of "these gigantic truths" leading to the personal and political reformation of morals. The indomitable joy that carries the day in time of temptation and trial is rooted in the cross of Christ. If we would fight for joy and endure to the end in our struggle with sin, we must know and embrace the full meaning of the cross.

> If we would . . . rejoice in [Christ] as triumphantly as the first Christians did; we must learn, like them to repose our entire trust in him and to adopt the language of the apostle, "God forbid that I should glory, save in the cross of Jesus Christ" [Galatians 6:14], "who of God is made unto us wisdom and righteousness, and sanctification, and redemption" [1 Corinthians 1:30].[125]

In other words, the joy that triumphs over all obstacles and perseveres to the end in the battle for justice is rooted most centrally in the doctrine of justification by faith. Wilberforce says that all the spiritual and practical errors of the nominal Christians of his age—the lack of true religious affections and moral reformation—

> RESULT FROM THE MISTAKEN CONCEPTION ENTERTAINED OF THE FUNDAMENTAL PRINCIPLES OF CHRISTIANITY. They consider not that Christianity is a scheme "for justifying *the ungodly*" [Romans 4:5], by Christ's dying for them "*when yet sinners*" [Romans 5:6-8], a scheme "for reconciling us to God—*when enemies* [Romans 5:10]; and for making the fruits of holiness *the effects, not the cause*, of our being justified and reconciled.[126]

---

[125] Ibid., p. 66.
[126] Ibid., p. 64. Emphasis added, but the capitalization is his emphasis.

Politician with a Passion for Pure Doctrine

It is a stunning thing that a politician and a man with no formal theological education should not only *know* the workings of God in justification and sanctification, but *consider them so utterly essential* for Christian living and public virtue. Many public people *say* that changing society requires changing people, but few show the depth of understanding Wilberforce did concerning *how* that comes about. For him, the right grasp of the central doctrine of justification and its relation to sanctification—an emerging Christlikeness in private and public—were essential to his own endurance and for the reformation of the morals of England.

This was why he wrote *A Practical View of Christianity*. The "bulk" of Christians in his day were "nominal," he observed, and what was the root difference between the nominal and the real? It was this: The nominal pursued morality (holiness, sanctification) without first relying utterly on the free gift of justification and reconciliation by faith alone based on Christ's blood and righteousness. "The grand distinction which subsists between the true Christian and all other Religionists (the class of persons in particular whom it is our object to address) is concerning the *nature* of holiness, and the *way in which it is to be obtained*."[127] What they do not see is that there must be a reconciliation with God and an imputed righteousness from him *before* we can live holy and righteous lives in the world. This was all-important to Wilberforce.

He saw that the nominal Christians of his day had the idea that "[morality] is to be *obtained* by their own natural unassisted efforts: or if they admit some vague indistinct notion of the assis-

---

[127] Ibid., p. 166.

tance of the Holy Spirit, it is unquestionably obvious on conversing with them that this does not constitute the *main practical
ground* of their dependence."[128] They don't recognize what con-
stitutes a true Christian—namely, his renouncing "with indigna-
tion every idea of attaining it by his own strength. All his hopes
of possessing it rest altogether on the divine assurances of the
operation of the Holy Spirit, in those who cordially embrace the
Gospel of Christ."[129]

This Gospel that must be "cordially" embraced (that is, with
the heart and affections, not just the head) is the good news that
reconciliation and a righteous standing with God precede and
ground even the Spirit-given enabling for practical holiness. "The
true Christian . . . knows therefore that this holiness is not to
PRECEDE his reconciliation to God, and be its CAUSE; but to FOL-
LOW it, and be its EFFECT. That, in short, it is by FAITH IN CHRIST
only that he is to be justified in the sight of God."[130] In this way
alone does a person become "entitled to all the privileges which
belong to this high relation," which include in this earthly life a
"partial renewal after the image of his Creator," and in the life to
come "the more perfect possession of the Divine likeness."[131]

Perhaps Our Greatest Need

Is it not remarkable that one of the greatest politicians of Britain
and one of the most persevering public warriors for social justice
should elevate doctrine so highly? Perhaps this is why the impact

---

[128] Ibid.
[129] Ibid.
[130] Ibid. Capitalization is his.
[131] Ibid.

of the church today is as weak as it is. Those who are most passionate about being practical for the public good are often the least doctrinally interested or informed. Wilberforce would say: You can't endure in bearing fruit if you sever the root.

From the beginning of his Christian life in 1785 until he died in 1833, Wilberforce lived off the "great doctrines of the gospel," especially the doctrine of justification by faith alone based on the blood and righteousness of Jesus Christ. This is where he fed his joy. Because of these truths, "when all around him is dark and stormy, he can lift up an eye to Heaven, radiant with hope and glistening with gratitude."[132] The joy of the Lord became his strength (Nehemiah 8:10). And in this strength he pressed on in the cause of abolishing the slave trade until he had the victory.

Therefore, in all our zeal today for racial harmony, or the sanctity of human life, or the building of a moral culture, let us not forget these lessons: Never minimize the central place of God-centered, Christ-exalting doctrine; labor to be indomitably joyful in all that God is for us in Christ by trusting his great finished work; and never be idle in doing good—that men may see our good deeds and give glory to our Father who is in heaven (Matthew 5:16).

---

[132] Ibid., p. 173.

Whatever was written in former days
was written for our instruction,
that through endurance and
through the encouragement of the Scriptures
we might have hope.
THE APOSTLE PAUL
ROMANS 15:4

Let us run with endurance
the race that is set before us,
looking to Jesus.
HEBREWS 12:1-2

CONCLUSION

The Imperfection and All-Importance of History

As I look back over what I have written, I feel ambivalent about it. On the one hand, it seems utterly provincial in view of the breadth and horror of the obstacles to endurance in many parts of the world today and in other cultures of that day. Here were three British men (how different some of the demands on women!), well-fed, well-clothed, living in the secure, comfortable, fast-developing, prosperously emerging modern world. The threats to their endurance were not beheading, burning at the stake, imprisonment, poisoning, starvation, torture, exile.

Not only that, when I consider the boundless resources in the Scriptures for our endurance, the scope of these chapters and these lives is very narrow. For example, consider the stupendous scope of Romans 15:4, "Whatever was written in former days was written for our instruction, that through *endurance* and through the encouragement of the Scriptures we might have hope." What this verse says is that *everything* written in the Bible was put there by God for the sake of our endurance—that no matter what our suffering, we might not lose *hope* but be encouraged to press on in faith.

So on the one hand, what I have written is historically and culturally narrow, and a mere fragment of the wealth of what God offers us for our endurance in the Bible. It is right and fitting for an author to say this and a reader to hear it. How finite and limited and fallible we are as humans! Banish all thoughts of finality or comprehensiveness or perfection. Finitude and fallenness will yield no final and comprehensive books or sermons. Those who claim otherwise simply have not counted the languages and cultures in the world and do not see how deeply we are corrupted by sin.

And consider also how little I have said about the *goal* of endurance! Endurance implies endurance *for* something. This is the main thing. We want to get there! Those who write poems and say memorable things about how the journey, not the destination, is the main thing simply have not tasted what Christians have tasted.

When you have tasted the Christian hope you don't say clever things about the glory of striving over arriving. You say that striving and enduring are worth it because they lead to "eternal life" (Matthew 19:29; John 12:25; Romans 2:7; Galatians 6:8) . . . that enduring is worth it because it produces a "weight of glory" (2 Corinthians 4:17) . . . that it's worth it because those who hold fast "inherit the promises" (Hebrews 6:12) . . . that those who endure persecution will receive a "great . . . reward" (Matthew 5:12) . . . that those who don't grow weary will "reap . . . in due season" (Galatians 6:9) . . . that those who make sacrifices "will be repaid at the resurrection of the just" (Luke 14:14) . . . that those who conquer will "eat of the tree of life" (Revelation 2:7) . . . and that "if in this life only we have hoped in Christ, we are of all people most to be pitied" (1 Corinthians 15:19).

Christians know that that there is joy on the journey. The Calvary road is not a joyless road. But we also know that this embattled joy flows from the hope we have in the future, and that if that future is cut off, the present taste of it is cut off. We are able to rejoice in the tribulations of this life for one reason:

they work *hope* (Romans 5:3-4). If the hope is vain, the joy vanishes. Sufferings are sufferable in joy because they are suffered in hope: "I consider that the sufferings of this present time are not worth comparing with the glory that is to be revealed to us" (Romans 8:18). Those who exalt striving over arriving have not suffered enough agony or seen enough of God. Christians endure not because life is good, but because death is gain.

How is it gain? What is the "life" and "glory" and "promise" and "reward" and "harvest" and "repayment at the resurrection" when we "eat of the tree of life"? The Bible leaves no doubt: It is Christ. Paul said, "To die is gain" and then said, "My desire is to depart and be with Christ." Christ was the gain. He "would rather be away from the body" because that would mean being "at home with the Lord" (2 Corinthians 5:8). But the decisive word is given by Jesus when he brought his prayer for all the saints to a climax with this petition: "Father, I desire that they also, whom you have given me, may be with me where I am, to see my glory" (John 17:24). Christ is the life and the glory and the promise and the reward and the harvest and the repayment at the resurrection and the tree of life.

Which is why the Bible says, "Let us run with endurance the race that is set before us, looking to *Jesus*" (Hebrews 12:1-2). Jesus Christ is the deepest root of endurance. Seeing and savoring him is the source of strength that keeps us striving against sin and Satan and sickness and sabotage.[1] And the place he is seen most clearly and most powerfully and most mercifully is in his massive achievement for us on the cross.

---

[1] This is so important for our survival as Christians that I wrote a book called *Seeing and Savoring Jesus Christ* with thirteen portraits of the Lord to help us see him for who he is and savor him for all he's worth (Crossway Books, 2001). We can't endure without "looking to Jesus."

This brings me now to the other side of my ambivalence about the present book. I said I feel ambivalent about what I have written because it is culturally and historically limited, and because it is biblically fragmentary compared to what God has provided for our endurance in his Word. But now, on the other hand, I say with joy and confidence that with all these limitations, what we have seen and heard from the lives of John Newton, Charles Simeon and William Wilberforce brings us finally, in each case, to the one main root of endurance. And I would venture the bold claim that this root transcends all cultures and all centuries, and that it sums up the whole Bible—namely, Christ crucified, risen, and reigning as the ground and goal of all our endurance.

If these witnesses, by their Christ-exalting endurance, help us see the glory of God in the face of the crucified Christ, then they will have served us well. These swans will not have sung in vain if we, by seeing and savoring Jesus Christ more clearly, do justice, pursue world missions, love our neighbors, care for the poor, seek the lost, and finish well.

A NOTE ON RESOURCES
DESIRING GOD MINISTRIES

Desiring God Ministries exists to spread a passion for the supremacy of God in all things for the joy of all peoples through Jesus Christ. We have hundreds of resources available for this purpose, most of which are books, sermons, and audio collections by John Piper. Visit our website and discover

- Free access to over twenty years of printed sermons by John Piper
- New, free, downloadable audio sermons posted weekly
- Many free articles and reviews
- A comprehensive online store where you may purchase John Piper's books, audio collections, as well as God-centered children's curricula published by DGM
- Information about DGM's conferences and international offices

Designed for individuals with no available discretionary funds, DGM has a *whatever-you-can-afford* policy. Contact us at the address or phone number on the next page if you would like more information about this policy.

DESIRING GOD MINISTRIES
720 Thirteenth Avenue South
Minneapolis, Minnesota 55415-1793

Toll free in the USA: 1-888-346-4700
International calls: (612) 373-0651
Fax: (612) 338-4372
mail@desiringGOD.org
www.desiringGOD.org

DESIRING GOD MINISTRIES
UNITED KINGDOM
Unit 2B Spencer House
14-22 Spencer Road
Londonderry
Northern Ireland
BT47 6AA
United Kingdom

Tel/fax: 011 (02871) 342 907
www.desiringGOD.org.uk
dgm.uk@ntlworld.com

INDEX OF SCRIPTURES

INDEX OF PERSONS

INDEX OF SUBJECTS